Early Praise for

I'm a Coal Miner's Daughter...But I Cain't Sang

"Though the history is painful, the end result isn't. It says, in an existential frame—I hurt, I struggled, I overcame. The book is about hope in the midst of struggle, not just a reflection on all things coal-mining. I recommend it highly."

"A great writer can make people laugh and cry and you have accomplished that. I read it aloud yesterday as we drove...and we laughed so hard that I even got tears in my eyes."

"[I've just started your book and] it has already made me laugh and cry so it's got to be good!! I love Momie Edna!!"

"It does present a true picture of how life was in the coal camps and awakened my memory about some things I had forgotten about."

"What an accomplishment and a legacy for your daughters and grandchildren!"

"...you told of so many things we can relate to whether you grew up in the mountains or not..."

"What a great read, especially having been raised in Kopperston...so many things to remind me of home and the people there."

I'm a Coal Miner's Daughter

BUT I CAIN'T SANG

Nadine Justice

I'M A COAL MINER'S DAUGHTER
But I Cain't Sang

by Nadine Justice

Cover Design and Artwork by Darryl Lankford
EPROM, Inc.

Excerpts in the Afterword from:

Appalachian VOICE, February/March 2012

The UMWA Journal, 1985

Open Salon, 2010
http://open.salon.com/blog/procopius/2010/01/30/
its_happening_now_the_2nd_battle_of_blair_mountain.html

Dedication

To the two most amazing women I know:
my daughters
Sherrie Hatfield Ferguson & Sandi Hatfield Jones

Contents

PREFACE

*These memoirs are simply "memory snapshots" that
have remained in my mind as significant milestones and
measurements of my life's journey.*

*Some of the stories were painful to write but others warm my
heart and have satisfied a longing to incorporate the person
I once was into the one I have become—a better me, I think.
During the process, I sometimes laughed and
sometimes cried—I think you may, too.*

*— Nadine Justice—
October, 2012*

Black Maria*

On a cold and dreary winter's day
In my mother's arms, I did rock and sway
And in the Coal Camp the whistle did sound
We knew no good news would be found.

Ol Black Maria! Please pass us by,
For I could not stand to see my mother cry.
Ol Black Maria! Please do not slow
For I could not bear my father to go.

The cries were heard throughout the camp,
Fire, rock and old black damp,
The demons of death were released that day.
The women on their knees began to pray,
Ol Black Maria! Please pass us by.

And on that awful, fateful day
Ol Black Maria did pass our way
And took another miner's soul
All for the digging of that old black coal.

—Eddie Ogle, singer/songwriter—

*"Black Maria" refers to the ambulance wives and children
dreaded to see coming through the camp.

COAL CAMP LIFE

*I*t's all over the news—another mining disaster, men trapped, voices heard, they're still alive. It's a race against time to dig them out before it's too late and the black earth they're buried in becomes their permanent graves. I can't seem to concentrate on anything else. I'm either glued to the television set or constantly checking the news for updates. All this emotional angst brings to surface fresh memories of a time long ago when I lived in a coal camp community.

I'm transported back in time to when I'm a little girl again, maybe four or five years old, and I can hear that "death whistle." How can a single sound raise the hair on the back of a little child's neck? Don't know what the grown ups called that awful sound but my name for it was the "death whistle," 'cause it meant somebody's daddy was dead or buried alive deep underground. Not sure exactly how old I was at this first recollection but already I knew how to pray, "Please God, don't let it be my daddy this time, especially not *my* daddy."

Before I was even born, my father, Curtis Justice, was the victim of a mining accident, in a coal mine in West Virginia, which cost him his left arm. He was only twenty-seven years old at the time. For several days after the accident he laid in a hospital bed in Charleston, West Virginia refusing to allow the doctors to amputate his withered black hand, until his brother, Emory, convinced him that he would die otherwise. After the amputation, he would undergo four unsuccessful operations designed to attach an artificial hand that was promised to look "realistic."

Each surgery took another inch of his arm, until finally it stopped just below his elbow. Realizing the futility of it all, he left the hospital without being officially released. Later he would say that he was convinced that, as long as he had been willing, the surgeons would have continued to experiment on him until it killed him.

Soon after the amputation, his pretty young wife left him and Dad moved back to Kentucky. It was rumored that she said she didn't want to be married to "a crippled man." A few years later, Dad's younger brother, Clyde, married my mother's older sister, Maggie. On a visit back home to her parents' house, my aunt brought out photographs of her brother-in-law. Mother is said to have made the comment that my father was the best looking man she had ever seen.

When this compliment was passed on to Dad, he was flattered and began writing notes to Mother. She quickly responded in kind. Mother's parents wouldn't allow her to date (she was only fifteen) but they managed to meet each other on the sly and decided to get married. Because Mother was underage, Aunt Maggie went to the courthouse with Dad and posed as the intended bride in order to obtain the marriage license.

On a Sunday morning, a few days later, before leaving for church with Momie Edna, Mom tossed her clothes out of an upstairs bedroom window, and according to plan, Maggie retrieved them. While Momie Edna was distracted by the preaching, Mother announced that she needed to go to the outhouse, and slipped out of the church. Dad was waiting for her outside.

The date was April 16, 1940. Dad was twenty-nine, soon to be thirty, and Mother was only half his age. My grandmother would tell me that story many times when I was growing up, crying as if it had only happened the day before. I later heard that Dad spent his wedding night in jail because Poppy had him arrested.

Pregnant soon after, Mother lost her first child, a baby boy, to miscarriage. She was seventeen when I was born and only one year older when my brother Haford came along. Times were hard and work in the mines was sporadic because of frequent strikes, but because Dad already owned a house and some land, my parents managed through farming and occasional odd jobs.

Even when work was available in the coal mines, the conditions were deplorable. Sometimes my father had to crawl on hands and knees, carrying his dinner bucket in his teeth by the bail, because the ceiling of the tunnel leading to the face of the coal was so low.

So, when Koppers Coal Company opened another huge modern mine in West Virginia, there was a mass exodus of ablebodied and experienced miners from eastern Kentucky. My family was among them.

Fearful that he might not be hired because of his handicap, my father was overly grateful to get such a good job. He never trusted the gossip that the foremen argued over who would get to have him in their crews, so he worked harder than anyone else until the day he retired, at age 62 with black lung disability. As a result, through all the years after we moved, though other miners were laid off for various reasons, my father was never without work.

There are not enough words or photographs in all creation to adequately convey the true essence of life in a coal camp. If you haven't lived it you can't know it. I cannot think of a more unique lifestyle. Somehow, living in close proximity to other coal mining families provided a feeling of normalcy and safety. Koppers Coal Camp, where we lived, was not typical, but the life of a coal miner was the same regardless of where you lived. Ours was a close knit community where everyone cared about their neighbors. We never heard of baby sitters and no one locked their doors. It wasn't uncommon for a mother to ask the next door neighbor to look after her children until she returned from grocery shopping.

I don't know what my parents would say if they were still alive, but I thought living in the coal camp was wonderful—my brother and I had an unlimited supply of playmates our own age and, unlike children today, the words "I'm bored" were not part of our vocabulary.

I remember once when my brother went missing and Mother, in a panic, began yelling out to the neighborhood that she couldn't find Haford. In what seemed like only seconds, a crowd had gathered and people dispersed in all directions to help in the search. As it turned out, the little fellow had just crawled behind the sofa and fallen asleep. When he finally awoke and was discovered, everyone laughed with relief and went on home.

There were many other benefits to living in Koppers Coal Camp, such as the Art-Deco-style company store which offered better quality goods than most locally owned retail stores. The company-owned school and medical facilities were readily available to the miners and their families, and were undoubtably the best around. The houses were new, clean, attractive, and were offered, at a very reasonable price, to all employees. My mother kept our house looking nice even though cleaning house was not something she enjoyed. I didn't know that about her until later when we moved away to the country and she neglected housework to tend the gardens.

As the oldest child and only girl, I had a room of my own with matching furniture. Mother dressed me in pretty homemade dresses and kept my hair shiny clean and curled. We didn't have store-bought hair curlers so she rolled swatches of hair around stretchy white anklets and tied the ends in knots. I didn't like sleeping with those lumpy socks tied in my hair but the results were actually quite good.

In addition to my clothes, she made doll clothes for all my dolls and transformed round oatmeal boxes into beautiful doll beds lined with satin and trimmed in lace. I never told her but occasionally I let my cat sleep in one of them.

On weekends, we usually had guests. After dinner, the adults would start a card game while the kids played together outside until well after dark. Yes, life was good but not easy…

We never saw my father with coal dirt on him because he always showered at the bathhouse before coming home from work—unless there was an accident at the mines. When that happened, we would hear a long loud whistle blast that struck fear in the hearts of the women and stopped the laughter of the children.

When the whistle was blown, the miners all knew to prepare to evacuate the mines—that there had been an explosion, a roof cave-in or the detection of methane gas. The bathhouse was only in operation after the end of each shift and in those times, there was no time for a bath anyway.

Everyone in the neighborhood came outside to watch and wait for the men to begin trickling home. Most of them caught rides with a co-worker or rode the bus, which dropped them off after work at the end of the street where they lived.

Our house was in the middle camp, which consisted of a long straight line of twenty-one houses, and ours was located at the far end. When the men got out of the vehicles they began walking but gradually picked up their pace, and some even broke into a run— as they approached their homes. With the black coal dust on their faces, they were not recognizable at a distance so as they came within earshot of their respective families, each man began shouting out his own name. Everyone stood frozen in place, listening.

Eventually, when most families were reunited, we would hear screams from the women and cries from the children whose fathers did not come home.

To this day, when I sit watching the news of coal mine disasters on TV, from the safety of my home, I can still hear the death whistle. I can see my father running and hear him say, "It's me, Nell Ruth. It's Curtis. I'm all right."

I hear the shouts of relief. And I still hear the screams for the husbands and fathers who will never come home.

COAL MINER'S DAUGHTER

*I*n spite of the risks and adversities, life in a coal camp community was a good life if you were fortunate enough to have a father who worked for Koppers Coal Company.

In Kopperston, West Virginia we never had any of the infamous union wars such as Bloody Harlan, which took place in Harlan County, Kentucky or the Matewan massacre in West Virginia. However, the necessity for striking to obtain a victory for the workers was a national event and our community was not immune. When a contract period between the coal companies and the United Mine Workers of America was nearing its end, the world had never seen the level of solidarity expressed by the body of coal miners.

John Llewellyn Lewis was a hallowed name in the world of coal mining; many miners even named their children after him. As a coal miner's daughter, the image of that big man with the bushy eyebrows, who was president of the UMWA, will be forever etched in my mind. In the early1940's every man, woman and child living in any coal camp community in America revered him as the savior. He fought for and won many advances for miners including higher roofs in the mines, better wages, hourly pay (instead of "pay by the load"), and various other precepts for safer working conditions. If when he was younger my father had been working at a union mine under the watchful eye of John L. Lewis, he might not have spent the better part of his life loading coal with one arm.

The term "Scab" referred to a person who betrayed his fellow miners and crossed the picket lines to work without a contract. Scabs were considered to be scum lower than common criminals but, sadly, sometimes a man would have to choose between the risk of being ostracized and perhaps even killed by his picketing peers, or letting his family starve.

Many families, like ours, had moved from Kentucky when Koppers opened that new mine and were friends before moving to West Virginia. They did their best to help each other when a strike was in process, and the times were hard. During a strike that lasted 56 days, I remember hearing stories about a family with several children who almost starved. By the time help arrived, in the form of garden vegetables and farm fresh milk, brought back to them from Kentucky by another miner's family, the only thing left in their pantry was a single can of corn.

Most coal companies offered credit to employees in the form of a money substitute called Scrip, a type of stamped currency, which could only be used at the respective company-owned stores. Sometimes a miner or his wife might, foolishly, draw out so much advance pay in the form of Scrip that their envelope on payday would be empty. The worst case scenario was to have a negative balance at the beginning of the next pay period. If there should be an untimely strike, the fate of that family was sealed. Fortunately my father did not believe in going into debt or credit for any reason. We didn't buy anything unless it could be paid for at the time of purchase, so we never found ourselves in that predicament.

During the calm times, when work was steady, we often made trips back to Kentucky. These took place late at night after Dad got off work. Mother missed her family and the home she left behind when we moved to West Virginia for Dad's better job. Dad probably preferred to stay home and rest after a hard week in the mines but he never objected. Many Friday nights would find us excitedly preparing for the trip back "home" to our old house and a good visit with our grandparents, Momie Edna and Poppy George.

Mother had the car packed and my brother and me dressed in our pajamas, ready to leave as soon as dad got home from the mines, where he worked second shift. We slept in the back seat as our parents took turns driving over the five mountains that separated Wyoming County, West Virginia and Pike County, Kentucky.

On one of those trips I woke up and listened to my parents' whispered conversation as we traveled through the dark night. Dad said "Did you see that animal that just crossed the road? What do you think it was?"

"I don't know, Curtis, but it looked like a fox to me."

I piped up, "No, it wasn't. That didn't look anything like a fox. Poppy George showed me a fox and it looked just like a little bitty ironing board."

A long, awkward silence followed until Mother burst out laughing and told Dad she realized what I was talking about. Poppy killed animals and tanned the hides to sell. He hung the boards with the stretched skins, on the sunny side of the smoke house to cure. When I asked what that funny looking board with the tail hanging from it was he had answered "It's a fox."

As soon as we hit the bumpy dirt road of John's Creek, Haford and I would wake up and shout "We're in Kentucky now." In our young minds, the road ended at our grandparents' house and they were the only people who lived there.

Unfortunately, when a contract between the union and the coal company ended, the calm also ended. A strike at the mines might last for only a few days, but it could go on for several weeks, depending on how successful negotiations were. During those turbulent times, my father would take us back to Kentucky where we were safe and could live off the land, with a little help from our grandparents.

We traveled on Saturday or Sunday. Dad dropped us off at our old house and immediately returned to West Virginia in order to be available the minute the strike was settled and the miners were called back to work.

I quickly learned that the night trips were far better than those during the day. That revelation came with painful clarity on our very first Saturday morning trip when we were coming out of a hair-pin curve and heading immediately into another one. I tried hard to focus on something in an effort to stave off nausea from motion sickness.

I understood why it was my brother and I who got sick—the adults were able to ride in the front seat. By the time Mother remembered to tell us to stop jumping around in the back of the car and advised, 'Don't look down, stare at something straight ahead," it was already too late.

I looked up and there on the side of a high, flat cliff, someone had painted "PREPARE TO MEET THY GOD" in giant letters. As we rounded the next curve, another sign read, "JESUS SAVES." Those were the days before Mother got religion but I had heard of those two guys— even knew their last names. Jesus' was Christ and God's last name was Damn. Mother spoke of them often.

Before we had descended the first mountain, my brother and I were bent over outside the car, losing our breakfast and begging Jesus to save us or just let us die before we approached the next mountain. No one had seat belts or air conditioned cars in those days and passersby, driving with their windows down, could be heard laughing at our pitiful condition. It made us feel a little better that payback for their ridicule often came on the very next mountain.

After that episode, Haford and I spent the remainder of the five-hour trip in a stupor, praying that the worst of it was over. Not sure if our altered state had been brought on by motion sickness or by fear from the implications of the life- sized cliff messages, all I knew was that I regretted having learned to read at such a young age.

Somehow, mother made those uncertain times seem more like an adventure than a means of survival. I missed my father but came to enjoy our daily routines. We worked in the garden, collected Polk salad, picked berries and gathered walnuts and hazelnuts. On cooler evenings the three of us walked along the rock filled creek bed near our old house picking up chunks of coal, which we burned in the fireplace to keep the chill at bay while we slept. There was no electricity in the old house but the warm light of oil lamps and a flickering fire was so much better than electric lights.

We either cooked evening meals at our house on the wood burning cook stove or walked down the dirt road and across a swinging bridge to eat supper with our grandparents. For the purpose of tormenting me, my brother would wait until we were dead center of the bridge—where there was no turning back— and begin jumping to make the bridge creak and swing harder. I was terrified of that rickety old footbridge and could never resist looking down at the creek below, remembering that I had not yet learned to swim. I had no idea how long it had been there but knew it was really old because the boards were weathered and uneven and the cables holding it up were covered with rust.

I quickly forgot my fear of the bridge when I walked through the screened door of my grandparents' house. It seemed that Momie Edna knew the exact moment we were coming because she was already making sugar cookies. Those awful hard things sold in stores were no comparison to her cake- like sugar cookies with thick soft centers and crisp browned edges. To this day, when I think of Momie Edna, I can smell her special sugar cookies. I still miss them both— her the most.

After dinner we helped with chores—closing up the chicken house, drawing fresh water from the well and washing dishes. While our mother and grandmother visited, my brother and I found time to play and get into a little mischief. We loved to explore the big upstairs sleeping loft. As soon as we started climbing up the high steps, Momie would yell out "Don't you younguns stomp the floor up there, you'll make the lights go out!" But at every opportunity I did just that and blamed it on my brother. They always believed me and I was pleased to see him in trouble. Their house had electricity but the lights were natural gas. Inside each globe was a thin membrane, somewhat like a balloon, which covered the flame. If the fixture was bumped or shaken, the membrane would touch the flame and collapse, making the light go out. This required either Momie or Poppy to get up on a chair or ladder, install a replacement mantel and relight the gas. I still feel guilty when I remember doing that but, at the time, I was focused on paying back my brother for the bridge incident. Not a smart thing because we had to traverse the bridge again on the way home.

My favorite times of all were the weekends because that's when Daddy came and a hoard of cousins arrived to play after church on Sunday. The presence of my cousins was a welcome distraction that made Daddy's imminent departure a little less painful.

On one of those Sunday afternoons, my cousins brought streamers of colored crepe paper, which I had never seen before. I tore strips of each color into small pieces, soaked them in water and poured the brightly colored water into various sized medicine bottles. I then lined them up in carefully placed rows on the window sill of the play house. I'm sure that little building wasn't intended for that purpose, it was probably an abandoned shed for the tractor, but I had staked a claim to it as mine and had taken ownership. I thought those bottles with the sun shinning through the colored water were the most beautiful and fascinating things I had ever seen. While the other girls were making mud pies and playing tag with the boys I was busy decorating the "play house."

I thought those times would never change, that the good life I knew then as a coal miner's daughter would go on forever.

I was wrong.

POPPY GEORGE

I'm guessing that I'm about eight years old and I'm sitting on my grandparent's porch. It's almost dark and the lightning bugs have just started their play time. I sit quietly because I know that soon Poppy George will come out onto the porch, sit down on the swing and begin picking his banjo. I have waited all day for this moment, as I do every evening when I'm staying there.

Poppy George was an eccentric man, talented and smart, but unlike my father in every way. My dad was a more serious man; Poppy was fun. Sometimes, if I didn't make a fuss about it, he also picked his banjo and sang. I especially loved one song, a ballad about a woman named "Rose Conley." In later years, I wondered if he wrote the song himself and if Rose Conley had been his girlfriend.

I most admired, even envied the men in my family. Even at the young age of eight, I thought that it was a much better deal in life to have been born male. While I sat on the porch watching fireflies and scanning the mountains well beyond the many acres of land Poppy owned, Momie Edna was always still working–doing laundry, cleaning up after supper, or stringing beans. Poppy found time to play; Momie Edna never did.

On Sundays, as far back as I can remember, Poppy would get all cleaned up and either walk or ride his horse up the road to see his girlfriend. I recall, on occasion, watching Momie trim the hair on the back of his neck as part of this Sunday ritual. She cooked, killed the chickens, gathered the vegetables and cleaned up, after feeding as many as thirty relatives, while he dressed up in his best suit. Sometimes we were late leaving for home but our presence didn't cause him a moments' hesitation. He dressed up and left without regard to anyone who might still be visiting, and went to see his "woman."

After our weekend visits we packed the car for the return trip and, as we drove away, I remember watching Momie Edna wave goodbye until we were out of sight. She waved with one hand and raised her white apron to her face with the other, as I waved back with my arm stuck out the rolled-down car window, I knew she was wiping tears. So was I.

A few miles further we passed a house that sat close to the road and I caught a glimpse of Poppy George sitting on another woman's porch. I don't know if he saw me. He didn't wave and neither did I. No one else in the car waved either, though I'm sure they saw him too. By the time I was a teenager I understood that what I had witnessed was not just a neighborly visit. Everyone knew but no one talked about it, at least not in front of them.

I don't think Poppy liked his female grandchildren. That is, at least not until us girls got old enough so that he could clearly determine if we were going to be, to him, pretty or ugly. If you were blessed in the looks department, you might get a little attention from him, but for the most part he wouldn't even acknowledge you. On the other hand, you couldn't be too bad if you happened to be a boy—the meaner you were the better, in his book. He was known in the family for cheering on the boys, but punishing the girls for doing exactly the same things.

I think I always understood, on some level, that my family was dysfunctional, even when I was a young child. It didn't matter then. I only knew that I loved them and they loved me, at least Momie Edna did. I was never very sure about Poppy.

Once I was older and he thought I was probably going to turn out okay, he began addressing me as "Sissy." I understood it as approval and knew I had finally arrived. He still called me Sissy long after I married and had children of my own. There were also a few other subtle ways that showed his favor. When he came in from the fields for the noon-day meal he always took his hat off and parked it on the back of one of the ladder-back chairs until he was ready to go back to work. He washed his hands, then the back of his neck, splashing a little extra cool well water onto his parched face— excess water ending up on the worn linoleum kitchen floor.

One day I couldn't resist the urge to put the hat on. When Momie saw me she said "You better take that off before he sees you. He doesn't like for anybody to mess with his hat!"

At that very moment he walked in, saw me, and said, "It suits you, Sissy. We'll have to get you one."

Poppy cussed, laughed, chewed tobacco, drank liquor and pretty much did as he pleased, whereas Momie only worked, worried, fussed and complained a lot. But I loved the two of them passionately—then, and even more now. And I both loved and despised those summers I spent in Kentucky with them.

Momie would make me wash canning jars for hours in the hot sun, saying that her hands were too big to go inside the jars and mine were just the right size. She took great pride in keeping her vegetable garden tidy, and required my help with keeping the weeds at bay. Her favorite expression was, "If you can find a weed in my garden, I'll eat your hat."

She boasted, too, that no one would ever find a speck of dirt or a hair in any of her food. If she knew anyone who owned a cat that was allowed to come into their house, she wouldn't eat from their kitchen even if she was starving.

In fact, the word would get around and at the "all day meetin'" and dinner on the ground" gatherings, folks would either avoid or frequent the tables prepared by a lady depending on her reputation for cleanliness. One thing was sure— all the country folk would say "let's eat at Ednie's table, 'cause you can eat off the floors at Ednie's house." (If you lived in Johns Creek, Kentucky and your name ended with an "a," it was generally pronounced as if it had been spelled "ie.")

I remember going to those annual meetings, which were held at the family cemetery. A long line of local preachers would take turns preaching, followed by a break for an hour or two of eating and visiting. (I haven't seen that many preachers in one place since.)

All the adults greeted the kids by guessing who their parents were. I can't count the times I heard, "Lord, how mercy, Ednie, I don't have to ask who that'n belongs to. She's the spittin' image of Curtis." I hated that when I was a little girl, but later thought it was a good thing to be compared, in any way, to my father.

Much later in life, I made regular trips back to Kentucky from West Virginia to visit my grandparents. In fact, some of the more memorable events involved my own children. Once, when my younger daughter and I were helping "string" beans, Momie handed a galvanized bucket to Sandi, who was four or five years old at the time, and asked her to take it "up yonder" and dump the strings out for the chickens, who loved to eat them.

A few minutes later, when I realized my child had not returned, I found her standing outside the screened door, turning the bucket back and forth by the bail, as she looked up and all around. When I asked her what she was doing, she replied with a question. "Where's yonder?" My poor grandmother just couldn't imagine how I could have raised a kid so "citified" that she didn't know the meaning of "yonder."

My children shied away from Poppy because they thought he was scary. My cousins say he was a mean old man. Maybe they're right— he did change in peculiar ways in his old age. But I mostly remember the good times. And I see him in a different light, especially when I walk into the bedroom at our mountain cottage and see that empty old rocking chair. Mother said Poppy bought it for Momie when she was pregnant with their first child. He had carried it home, walking for miles because it would be impossible to carry it riding on a horse, and he didn't yet have a wagon. It's a crude old thing, carved from oak, but seeing it always makes me smile and know that he couldn't have been all bad.

During the last few years of Poppy's life, before he was diagnosed with Alzheimer's disease, I occasionally stayed with him so Momie could visit for a week or so with one of their grown children. Every evening after supper, Poppy would sit for hours on the long bench behind the homemade table telling me stories from his youth. He nearly always began with, "Sissy, did I ever tell you about......" Invariably, it would be a story I had heard many times, but I didn't remind him. I wanted to hear it again.

He had a lot of stories to tell. He had been a Blacksmith, a logger, a farmer, a musician and a barber. In addition to being a pretty good banjo picker, he made beautiful banjos. People would wait a year or more to get one of Poppy's hand-made banjos.

I loved hearing about his logging experiences. He told me they cut logs from trees on his land and tied them together, making a raft, which they then floated upon down the 99 mile long Johns Creek to a sawmill. He said when their raft came into view that the men, waiting at the sawmill, began whooping out excited shouts of greeting. After celebrating their safe arrival and visiting with the other men, he rode his horse home, which one of his grown sons had brought to meet him. As I listened to his story I could tell that he missed those good times.

One of his favorite stories was about how he drank whiskey and rode his horse on Saturday nights while Momie Edna went to church. He said that she and the preacher kept pestering him about coming to church, so one Saturday night he decided to go. He'd gotten drunk and rode his horse into the church and right down the middle of the aisle. Upon finishing the story, he would always laugh and slap his leg.

"And Sissy," he would say, "they never invited me back."

MOMIE EDNA

*I*have many wonderful memories of summers with my grandmother—some sad, some happy, some funny—but the importance of our relationship and the way it affected the quality of my life is immeasurable. I didn't have a good relationship with my mother but Momie Edna gave me a constancy that was otherwise lacking.

The house my grandparents lived in was originally a three-room log cabin where Poppy was born. It was later covered with siding to provide better insulation. To get to the house from the dirt road we had to open a wooden gate large enough for the car to pass through. We then parked the car by the barn and walked past Poppy's blacksmith shop on the way in. A second gate opened into the dirt yard leading up to the front porch, which was graced with metal chairs and gliders, and one coveted swing. Papaw trees, lining the nearby fence that protected Momie's garden, offered a sweet aroma when the fruit ripened. Located near the back of the house was a covered well with a pulley and wooden bucket. Beyond the well there was another fenced lot and a large chicken house. Closer to the house sat two more weathered buildings—one was a smokehouse and the other was used as Momie's canning house.

I remember one day when I was playing in the dirt yard when I was about six years old. Momie had expressly asked that I stay away from her setting hen because the chicks were almost ready to hatch and she didn't want the hen disturbed. There was a wooden box attached to the side of the smoke house where the chicken was keeping her eggs warm, and the box was just at eye level for me if I stood on my tiptoes. Naturally, my curiosity got the best of me and, when Momie wasn't looking, I crept over for a close-up look.

What she had neglected to tell me was that a setting hen gets really mad if anyone gets within threatening distance of her eggs. At the exact moment I managed to raise myself up to look in, the chicken stuck her head over the side of the box and pecked me on the nose. Needless to say, it wasn't an option for me to stay quiet (and therefore out of trouble) since I needed help to clean up my then bloody nose.

I don't remember exactly how old I was when it all began, but the nightly ritual of braiding my Momie Edna's hair and washing her feet would provide some of my dearest memories of time with her and solidify our bond. Momie Edna had long gray hair which she wore in a bun during the day but she combed and braided it before going to bed each night. In later years, her arthritis was so severe that it became hard for her to handle the braiding of her hair and was unable to bend down and wash her own feet. I knew, even as a young girl, that she would never have crawled into bed on her clean, line dried sheets with dirty feet.

Every night I was there I filled a metal pan with water and heated it on the old wood-burning cook stove, and then placed it on the wide plank floor in front of her chair. She would soak her feet as we talked and I braided her hair. When I was done with her hair, I would take her feet out of the warm soapy water and dry them, and then proceed to cut her toenails. Sometimes her feet were in such horrible condition, mostly from neglect, that I would have to apply several layers of lotion to try and alleviate the dryness.

I don't recall how we got onto the subject but, one night, Momie decided to give me a lecture on "how to keep my man happy." She began, in a round-about way, to tell me that no matter how I actually felt about it, I should still take care of my husband's needs, even if I didn't like "it."

I wasn't sure how to respond, but I told her that it was okay, because I actually liked "it." Surprised, she looked at me and said, "You do? Well, tell me about it."

I was taken aback by the fact that I was having a conversation about sex with my grandmother, and I think I said something like, "Well, everyone likes being kissed and hugged, and when you're married, 'that' is just part of it."

She told me that she so wished she had liked "it" because, if she had, then maybe Poppy wouldn't have taken a girlfriend. She cried as she told me how she loved him more than all of her seven children but had never liked "that." She explained that her mother had taught her only bad women liked "that." She thought by not liking it, she was just being a good girl.

She said when she learned about Poppy George's girlfriend she'd wanted to die at first, but that later in life, when there had been so much work to do, she had been just plain too tired. "Since he wanted to do it three or four times a night," she explained, "I was kinda glad for the help. And after having seven children, I was relieved that I didn't have to worry about "that" any longer, either."

Her revelation brought to mind a memory of when as a 14-year-old girl. I had sneaked upstairs to look through the treasures she kept in a big wooden quilt box. I came across what appeared to be a recent black and white picture of a very handsome young man, I was so excited that I ran downstairs with the picture, completely forgetting that I would be in trouble for having been in the forbidden storage box. I declared that was the best looking boy I had ever seen and wanted to know who he was and where he lived. Momie looked at the photo I was holding up, and smiled for a long minute. "That's your Pap when he was seventeen. I thought he was the best looking boy I had ever seen, too."

Our nightly talks took place in the front room, where there was a fireplace with a gas heater inserted. Ladder back chairs sat in a half circle in front of the fireplace. Momie's rocking chair was placed further away from the heat to the right and facing the front door. The fireplace mantle held a clock that ticked loudly and chimed on the half-hour. I don't know how they slept with that noisy thing, but they did. The clock was a necessary fixture in their daily lives because Momie could hear it from her vegetable garden. The strike of eleven-thirty signaled her to come inside and prepare the noon day meal, which they called dinner, before Poppy came in from the fields. (I now have that old mantle clock on a shelf in my mountain cottage). The room served as both a bedroom and sitting area and contained two double size feather beds. (In later years a hospital bed was added and placed by a window where Momie slept.) There was one large room upstairs with three or four beds where their children had once slept.

I thought those big white feather beds were the most beautiful beds I had ever seen. I could never figure out how Poppy, who chewed tobacco even in his sleep, managed to spit over the side without choking or staining the bed. But he did, and Momie emptied his spittoon every night and placed it in the middle of spread-out newspapers.

When I was still a young child they built a two-room addition onto the right side of the house which they continued to call "the new rooms" more than twenty years later. One was a bedroom and the other was a parlor where we all gathered around the tree to exchange gifts at Christmas time. Otherwise, the new rooms were only used for guests. They had a separate entrance accessible only by going out the back door of the kitchen or through a door off the front porch. When I was an adult and went for visits, everyone knew not to bother putting their stuff in the "new rooms" because they were reserved for me and mine. The only exception was my uncle Homer, who was Momie's youngest and favorite son.

Many other fond memories are of times spent in Momie's kitchen. We baked a cake or made sugar cookies almost every evening. I also "spelled" Momie with the chore of churning the milk into buttermilk. There was a peculiar art in learning how to plunge the dasher with just the right touch so that little milk was wasted and splashed onto the worn linoleum floor. The kitchen was a long, narrow room that ran the entire length across the back of the house. The furnishings consisted of an enormous homemade table set against a wall of windows, surrounded with a long bench on the window side and ladder back chairs on the other three sides. Between the cook stove and the table stood what Momie called a "stand table" that provided space for a metal water bucket and dipper, a wash pan, and a cake of her special lye soap.

Opposite the cooking area was a tall cabinet with a metal slide-out counter under a flour bin. (The top and bottom cabinets and drawers contained baking supplies.) Immediately to the right of that two-story cabinet was a waist-high three-drawer oak chest that held aprons and linens. (I also have that piece of furniture in my mountain cottage.)

I was an adult by the time my husband and brother built a new bathroom for my grandparents. I was never so relieved and happy as that day—as a child, I had to go to the outhouse, which involved unlocking and passing through a big gate that led into the field where the horses were kept.

I have no idea why they chose that location, but for some reason, I seemed to be the only person afraid to enter the horse lot. I was petrified of the horses and filled with dread each time I felt a need to go to the bathroom, especially at night. Naturally, the horses sensed my mood and I was the only person they chased. It was just one more good reason to wish I had been born a boy, because the boys simply walked outside at night and peed off the porch!

I continued the ritual of washing Momie Edna's feet and braiding her hair whenever I was able to be with her. Long after I had children of my own, I still went back to Kentucky to visit her, and as soon as my daughters were fast asleep in the "new rooms" I would go back into the main house and find my grandmother sitting in her rocking chair, dressed in her nightgown, patiently waiting for me.

My grandfather passed away at age 75, but Momie lived to be 89. During the last few years of her life, when her health began to fail, she went to live in Ironton, a small town in Ohio near the West Virginia border, in a house next door to her oldest daughter, my aunt Eunice.

At one point she was admitted to a hospital in Huntington, West Virginia, only two hours from my home, which was then in Beckley. During her hospital stay, I awoke in the middle of the night in a cold sweat because I had dreamed that she died. I immediately called the hospital to check on her, and instead of going back to sleep I got up and ready to visit her the following day.

When I arrived at the hospital she seemed fine. As usual, she was glad to see me and eagerly introduced me to all the nurses. "Come here," she said. "I want ya'll to meet my granddaughter. This is the best little girl you'll ever meet." Though I was almost 40 years old, she talked about me as if I had still been a child.

During my visit she told me that in the night, her heart had stopped beating and they had resuscitated her. Angry about the interference, she complained to me. "If you had been here," she said, "you wouldn't have let them do that to me." She was right.

Momie described the details of her near-death experience. Passing through an opening, maybe a gate, she was greeted by her oldest son, who had died a year earlier, and all the relatives who had gone before. She found her parents and her sisters and was ecstatic to see them. "But, honey," she said, "I looked all around and couldn't find your pap anywhere." I didn't have the heart to tell her that I was pretty sure Poppy George hadn't been there.

Momie was soon released from the hospital and lived at least another year. For her 89th birthday, my cousin Georgia Marie and I made plans to go and visit her. Though that morning there was a terrible snow storm, I assured my cousin that I was a careful driver and that my car, at that time a beautiful gold Mercedes, was stable on slick roads, so we made the trip, though it took twice as long as it would have under normal conditions. It was late when we arrived and most had decided we weren't coming. When we walked in the door of Momie's little house, I heard her say, "I told you all she would come."

My mother had come several days before, but because of the heavy snowfall had not ventured out to buy the necessary supplies to properly celebrate Momie's birthday. I quickly volunteered and Georgia Marie agreed to accompany me. My aunt Eunice, in spite of the fact that she owned the house Momie was living in, a big, beautiful home next door, nearly five hundred acres of land and a few other rental properties, was notoriously "frugal." I have no idea how she managed to do it but somehow, she'd arranged to get food stamps, which she wanted us to use to buy the groceries. Just as Georgia Marie and I were about to leave, Eunice interrupted. "I'll go because Nadine would be embarrassed to use food stamps," she said. I assured her that since I didn't live in Ironton, I could not have cared less. Shrugging her shoulders, she handed me the food stamps and we struck out again on the snow covered roads.

As we were checking out, the clerk stopped us when my bottle of wine came down the belt. "I'm sorry, Ma'am," she said, "but you can't buy alcoholic beverages with food stamps."

"Why not?" I asked. "That's how I got this fur coat." (I thought Georgia Marie would hurt herself laughing. I was wearing a fur coat with a hood.)

Upon our return, my cousin began apologizing to my tee-totaling grandmother. "I told her not to buy that wine," she said.

Momie's answer was quick. "That's all right," she said. "The Bible says a little wine is good for the stomach."

In retrospect, I think the truth of it was that if *I* did it, Momie would approve. For instance, the first time I went to see her after marrying my second husband, in one of our evening talks, she said, "Honey, they tell me you got married again."

"Yes, I did, Momie."

"Well," she responded, "I think that's just fine. And if this one doesn't work out, then get you another one and keep trying until you find a man that suits you."

Unfortunately, I took her advice.

I can still picture us, and the way the old house looked on those long ago nights, as clearly as if it had happened only last night. I still miss Mommie Edna. But regardless of any hardships I have experienced throughout my life I have always been comforted by the knowledge that one person loved me unconditionally.

It is more than enough.

ANGEL BROTHERS

"Why are all those people standing in our living room talking in whisper soft voices?" I thought. Then I heard someone say, "He's an angel now."

I cautiously stepped further into the room and saw the object of their attention. In the center was a small, white, box-like bed on a white stand. Inside the bed was a beautiful doll dressed in white baby clothes. He didn't look like an angel to me. He looked like one of my dolls but, unlike my used dolls, he was perfect.

No one seemed to be aware of me nor did anyone explain what was happening. I was mesmerized by how perfect and beautiful that baby doll was. I was not told "don't touch" and no one was watching, so I inched forward and put one small finger on his face. I don't remember how it felt to touch him but, somehow, I realized that he was neither angel nor baby doll. The pretty white box was not a doll bed—it was a coffin. He was my brother—and he was dead.

In my next memory snapshot, I am standing outside a circle of people who have gathered beside an open grave. My mother still has not acknowledged me. She is sitting on a large rock holding her head in her hands. I don't see tears so I think she is sick—that's what she always did when she was sick or had a headache.

I'm not sure when or how I learned that there was another baby who was still alive in a hospital two hours away. All I knew was that someone had awakened my brother and me in the middle of the night and whisked us away to our uncle's house. Mother had actually given birth to twin boys. The first baby who died weighed four pounds and the one still clinging to life weighed only a little more than two pounds.

I remember going with my dad and Uncle Joe to see my other brother. We stood outside a window to look in at him as he lay in an incubator with tubes attached to his tiny limbs. My dad cautioned me not to put my face on the glass. "Touch nothing," he said. "It's a hospital, and there are germs everywhere."

During the weeks my other baby brother was in the hospital, I don't think Mother ever went along to see him. When I was older and asked her why, she said, "Well, I didn't expect him to live and thought it best he didn't, because I knew that he could never be normal. It was best for him."

He tried to live. He hung on almost two months without ever being held by his own parents. I never had even a chance to get to know either of my brothers but I felt a loss even then. I still miss them to this day.

Nearly all my relatives have since moved away from Kopperston, West Virginia, or they've died, but I continue to feel strong ties to the place, because that is where my twin brothers are buried. I have never understood why I was more deeply affected by the births and deaths of those babies than other members of my family, but I was.

On rare trips back to the coal camp where I lived as a child, I check on the condition of the cemetery and pause before their graves. The tombstone is one unit for both graves and has lambs at the top on each side. They're still standing and in good condition except that the little lambs, once pink, have faded to gray.

A few years ago, my younger sister told me a story which put that event and Mother's unexplained attitude into better perspective. She said Mom had told her that she had always blamed herself for the twins' premature births and deaths. Angry with our father, she had begun a cleaning campaign, over- taxed herself, and went into early labor. I had never heard her talk about them or seen her shed tears over their deaths, but my sister said she cried and cried when she told her that story.

After mother passed away my siblings and I cleared out her house and divided up her personal belongings. It seemed appropriate that I later found, in one of the boxes I took, an old much-worn black purse—a thing that appeared to be trash. When I examined the contents of the purse, I found a receipt for what appeared to be my parents' first furniture purchase, Dad's UMWA membership card, and the birth certificates for my twin baby brothers. I believe it was divinely destined for me to have those tangible mementos. Though I was never able to hold either of them in my arms, I have carried my angel brothers in my heart for more than sixty years.

AUNT BECKY'S STORE

*W*hen I stepped out of a bright, cold October day in 1972, and into the warmth of Husein's Market, the sounds and smells that greeted me were unmistakably familiar. I had an overwhelming sense of having been there before, but I had only arrived in that country a few days earlier. As the contents of the darkened room gradually came into focus, I understood and was instantly transported back in time to a simple and innocent scene from my childhood.

I glanced over at my cousin, Bonnie Jean, and the cloud of dust she was kicking up from the dirt road. I couldn't help thinking of how glad I was that, unlike her mother, mine had allowed her cousin, Georgia Marie, to name me. I shuddered at the possibilities as I reflected on the name my mother had hung on my poor brother, Haford. I was equally grateful that Georgia Marie hadn't been able to come up with a name to go with Nadine, which she'd "borrowed" from her college roommate.

In rural Kentucky in those days, your middle name, reduced to an initial, didn't just serve to give dignity to your signature. Oh, no, they called you by both names. I had relatives with names like Phyllis Faye, Dottie Lou, John Eddie, Edna Marie and Ola Mae. Mother's name was Nell Ruth and I never once heard my father address her in any other way. Georgia Marie had saved me from that fate!

On this particular hot July afternoon, Bonnie Jean and I had just finished our chores for Momie Edna and were hell bent for Aunt Becky's store to spend our hard-earned nickels on sugar candy. We had looked forward to this all day, as we always did when we happened to visit our grandparents at the same time. We worked together to help them out yet still found time to have some fun of our own—not an easy thing to pull off in that atmosphere.

Bonnie Jean was pounding the dirt road and I was expending equal energy trying to keep up without getting dirty—I didn't want her to walk in the door of the store one second ahead of me, but I hated being dirty.

I loved Aunt Becky's dilapidated old store. It had never seen a paint brush and over the years had weathered to myriad shades of brown and gray. Three or four wide plank steps led up to the porch where it wasn't unusual to step over at least one sleeping hound dog on the way in.

The old building set just off the road to the left of Uncle Clarence's and Aunt Becky's house. Though they were actually a half mile away, they were my grandparents' "next door" neighbors; in the country, that was close enough. They were also kin—Clarence was Momie Edna's brother and Becky was Poppy George's sister. Their children were my mother's double first cousins—one was a boy, the other a girl, my sainted Georgia Marie. I was never quite sure what Uncle Clarence did for a living—I don't recall ever seeing him work in the fields like Poppy did.

Aunt Becky was a storekeeper. On slow days, one could hear the screen door slam behind her and catch a glimpse of her making her way from their house to the store hurrying to greet a potential customer. She had a sixth sense that told her when someone approached—there was no bell to alert her. She never missed a sale—not even ones as minuscule as our five-cent purchases—and it was said that Aunt Becky was as "tight" as the bark on a tree. But that was never my opinion of her.

On Saturdays, the store brimmed with activity. Women shopped and gossiped and old men sat on porch benches, talking politics and bragging about who had the best coon dog. Between sentences, the men would spit long streams of tobacco juice off the porch into the dirt below without ever acknowledging that too, was a competition.

As I stepped inside, it took my eyes a moment to adjust in the dimly lit room. The only light came from one small window on the back wall and two or three naked light bulbs. These could be turned on and off by pulling on a long string of twine attached to short chain located near the respective bulb.. Interspersed between the light bulbs hung an equal number of fly paper spirals speckled with their long dead victims.

I was always pleasantly assaulted by unusual aromas: stale ashes in the pot-bellied stove in the center of the room, foodstuffs like pinto beans, potatoes, coffee and rice packed in burlap sacks, and small bottles of cinnamon oil sat on a shelf waiting for the next lady making apple butter. The sacks lined the floor in front of glass-front merchandise cabinets, sharing space with kegs of various size nails.. The cabinets themselves were packed with knives and kitchen gadgets—rolling pins, flour sifters, and pie pans made of tin.

An ancient red soft drink cooler stocked with RC Cola, Orange Crush and Coca-Cola sat under the window. All the drink bottles were suspended by their caps from metal tracks. The shelves on the wall behind the counters were lined with rows of canned goods, baking powder and soda, sugar, flour and, of course, various brands of chewing tobacco with colorful names like "Red Man" and "Brown Mule."

Poppy would sometimes ask us to pick up some "backer" for him and have Becky put it on his account. Though we were young, no one ever questioned us about it; nor did they hesitate to sell us those boxes of long-stemmed matches that would "strike on any surface," from the soles of your shoes to a flat rock.

On the other side of the store was a wall of post office boxes that always fascinated me. Rumor had it that Aunt Becky, when bored, would steam open letters, read them, glean whatever juicy gossip she could, and then reseal them, assuming no one would be the wiser.

The counter tops were graced with huge apothecary jars filled with pickled eggs, peanuts, Nabs, beef jerky and the prized sugar candies that drew Bonnie Jean and me there—candies that came in all sizes and shapes from hearts to animal figures, featuring every color in the rainbow.

When I walked up to the counter and proudly plopped down my nickel, my eyes always grew wide as I watched Aunt Becky send scoop after scoop into the bag I was holding. The first time I went there I expected, based on Becky's reputation, only a few pieces of candy and was sure it wouldn't be enough to include all the colors and shapes. I guess she wasn't so stingy after all.

Eventually, as I got older and bolder, I became more enterprising and in order to increase the portions even more, I counseled Bonnie Jean in entrepreneurship. I had learned from listening to gossip between the grown-ups that there was a fierce competition between Aunt Becky and Burly Blackburn, who owned another store just up the road. After we had each consumed a few pieces of our candy I would take a nickel I had saved from a previous day's pay for washing canning jars and head on up to the Blackburn country store. I took my candy and mixed it with Bonnie's to form a heaping bag full. I showed it to Burly and said "Look how much candy Becky gave Bonnie Jean for just a nickel." He would then fill a bigger bag for me. Of course, I always took the larger "half" when I poured the candy from her bag back into mine.

A car horn outside jarred me from my reverie. Many years had passed since those days, and I was a long way from Kentucky—across the ocean where my husband's job had taken us and our two children. It hadn't been easy for them to fill the Turkish government's requirement that only men with wives and children be hired to work there, so George's boss Hank, and his wife Ella, went out of their way to make us comfortable. We had encountered a few hitches when we'd arrived and they were afraid we might leave them—before we'd even settled in—with the laborious prospect of finding replacements. They tried extra hard to present the town of Zonguldak in the best possible light.

Ella picked me up and took me on a tour of the town and naturally showed me the most impressive areas first. I was enamored with the bustling activity of the open market—the colorful fruits and vegetables and the abundant fresh fish from the Black Sea. Young men darted throughout the bazaar serving small glasses of complimentary hot tea as Ella, in broken Turkish, showed me how to negotiate with the vendors. I could tell that my own negotiating skills would serve me well there. Awed by the beauty of the marketplace, I felt both comforted and welcomed by the extraordinary hospitality of the Turkish people.

Uneasy about what I would think of the store where everyday staples could be found, Ella had saved Husein's Market for last. But when we'd climbed out of her car and entered the dingy old one-room store, I could hardly believe my eyes. Except for the many varieties of cheese and olives, I was standing in the beloved country store of my childhood. "Oh, it's Aunt Becky's store," I exclaimed. "I love it!" Ella breathed an audible sigh of relief.

I would visit Husein's Market many times while we were there, and before long, others began to call it "Aunt Becky's," too. Karhamon, our driver, who picked up our groceries on days we entertained, would look at the list and then at me. "Aunt Becky's?" he would ask. and I would smile. "Evet, teşekkür ederim." *Yes, thank you.*

That wonderful, dingy little store would prove to give me a small piece of home and offer a sense of belonging in what otherwise might have felt like a very foreign place.

By the time we left Zonguldak, almost two years later, our housekeeper Hatiçe, most of our Turkish friends, and the few other American families in town all referred to Husein's Market by the nickname I had given it. From what I've been told, they did for a long time after.

ONE-ROOM SCHOOLHOUSE

*W*hen I was eight or nine years old, Mother had a notion to move out of the coal camp and find a place to raise farm animals and plant vegetable gardens. She said she was tired of having neighbors in her back door and wanted to be in the country again, where she could have some privacy.

The abandoned farmhouse she found for us was located four miles up in a hollow accessible only by an unpaved dirt road. It was situated in a valley between two mountains and included 55 acres of land, 25 of which were level enough for pastures and crops. The remaining acreage was mostly hillside.

My brother Haford used to tell people that he and Dad planted potatoes on one plot that was so steep that, at harvest time, they only had to dig the bottom row and the rest of the potatoes just rolled down. He also said that, at milking time, all he had to do was look up the chimney to check and see if the cow was coming home.

Mother joked that the tin roof was so full of holes that, when it rained, she and Dad had to sleep *under* a rubber sheet instead of *on* one like other couples with babies. I never saw the humor in any of that.

In spite of being closed in between two mountains, which made me claustrophobic, I didn't hate the place immediately. In fact, for the first few months, before it dawned on me that the move would be a permanent one, I was entertained by this new and unfamiliar place.

For instance, shortly after we moved and I was exploring outside, I broke some branches with beautiful blossoms off a tree—enough for a large bouquet—and proudly presented them to my mother. She thanked me and put them in a wide-mouthed Mason jar filled with water.

A short time later, unsatisfied with what I perceived as a lack of enthusiasm for my gift, I said, "Mother, you didn't act like you really liked the flowers I brought you." After a long pause, she responded, "I *do* like them, Nadine, but I would have liked them even better later in the summer. Then they would have been peaches."

My favorite memory is of Priscilla and Have Rollins, an elderly couple who lived on the way to and from school. Before our parents organized the farm and the house, and acquired chickens and a cow, my brother and I were given the chore of stopping on the way home to buy milk and eggs from them.

I don't know how old the Rollins' were, but in retrospect, I'm sure they were older than my grandparents, and I loved being in their neat and beautifully furnished home. The kindness and respect they showed each other was a rare thing to behold—theirs seemed to be a "perfect" marriage.

The house was an old farmhouse like ours and not especially grand in and of itself, but when they invited us to come into their parlor and sit down to visit the aura around them was intoxicating to me.

Haford and I stopped there twice a week and every visit was as special to me as the first. Mrs. Rollins would ask us polite questions about school and our family's well-being, Mr. Rollins would go over to the covered glass candy jar on the mantle and take out a peppermint candy for each of us. Only then would they give us the milk and eggs, take our money and send us on our way home.

It was clear by the way they spoke to each other that this old married couple were still in love. Because they were of German descent, I assumed the love they showed toward each other was just a cultural characteristic and not something I should expect as part of *my* home life. I had never witnessed anything like that with anyone in *my* family, though I certainly wanted it for myself.

The milk came in a big glass gallon jar and the eggs were wrapped in pieces of newspaper which were then stuffed into a brown paper bag. It wasn't easy to walk the remainder of the distance home keeping the milk from shaking too hard and being churned into buttermilk. Nor was there any guarantee that my brother would get the eggs home without breaking at least half of them. I knew we would get into trouble if that happened. I walked slowly, not out of concern for our fragile cargo, but because I was busy reflecting on the vision of Mr. and Mrs. Rollins. Sometimes the day was sinking toward dusk by the time we arrived home.

As if the extreme change in home life wasn't traumatic enough, it was our new school situation that nearly did me in. In the Coal Camp, we had been enrolled in a modern and lively school with lots of students and highly qualified teachers. Haford and I both excelled there. When we moved to the country, we were transferred into a one room school, where there was only one teacher for all eight grades, and supplies were equally scarce. The building, already old with peeling white washed siding, had no indoor plumbing.

The only bright spot, at the otherwise awful Craney One-Room School, was Miss Adams, a young woman trying to make the best of her teaching debut. I'm sure she had no idea what she was getting into when she accepted the position. Even so, I think she tried to create some semblance of order and did a pretty good job considering what she had to work with.

Miss Adams enjoyed some small successes because she was really pretty, and the older boys—especially bullies like "Tall Leonard,"—wanted to please her. (A glance at the photo at the beginning of this story will explain the nickname.)

Girls liked Miss Adams, too, because she was young and beautiful and had long, dark, wavy hair. I especially loved her strappy high-heeled shoes, which she told me were called espadrilles, and coveted her fashionable clothes. I could hardly wait to be old enough to wear clothes and shoes like hers and to paint my nails red.

There's no doubt that adding two new students late in the term wreaked havoc on an already fragile classroom equilibrium. In an effort to make her work load easier and instruction more efficient, Miss Adams decided to reorganize the classes and combine some of the grades—an effort which nearly cost me in a way that could have changed my life forever. I was the only student on my grade level, and she decided to ask for permission to put me back with my brother in a grade level one lower than mine. I'm sure the solution seemed obvious, and easily done, so she sent a message to my mother and asked her to come in for a conference.

I'll never forget seeing my mother sitting in one of the school desk chairs waiting for our teacher to finish a lesson and talk to her. She looked so shy, nervous and ill-at-ease, but she was there to stand up for me. The same woman who never attended a PTA meeting throughout my childhood came to my rescue that day. I understood what it cost her and I will always be grateful to my mother for that.

When Miss Adams presented her plan, my mother asked for, and received, confirmation that I was still making good grades. She refused to give her consent. Instead, she suggested the alternative—that my brother be moved up one grade level to join me. Under no circumstance would she allow me to be held back.

Miss Adams deferred to my mother's wishes and my brother and I stayed in our grade levels. We finished the school year with only a few minor incidents, most of which involved Tall Leonard. Over the summer, Haford got a pony, Mother worked in her garden and doted on my baby brother Shawny, and Dad planted crops for the animals, but I did not fare so well.

I began to feel as if I would surely suffocate between those mountains. Feeling isolated and alone, I moped about, daydreaming and biding my time until the summer was over and we returned to school.

That fall, my idol, Miss Adams, was gone. She had left to get married and would not return. In her place was a middle-aged preacher with an angry countenance and dour disposition. The schoolhouse looked abandoned and had not been cleaned inside or out. In fact, not a single effort had been made in preparation for the children's new term.

Grass sprouted up through the steps leading into the school like unwanted thoughts. Out in front, the few parking spaces and small yard were the only playground we had and, because of the remote location, had served as a lover's lane all summer. It would be a long time before I learned what a condom was but, even then, I understood that what the first graders were picking up off the ground and blowing into long balloons were not play things. Judging by the look of disgust on the teacher's face I could see that it was something bad, but he kept his distance and made no effort to intervene. He simply looked on as the older boys snickered and the first graders continued searching for more "balloons."

I could hardly believe our lovely young woman teacher had been replaced by that awful old slack-jawed man. It was immediately clear that the old preacher teacher had no business teaching at all, but especially young children because he made no effort to protect them.

The bully, Tall Leonard, instantly picked up the scent—the good behavior he had feigned the previous year to impress Miss Adams was no longer required, and his cruelty manifested itself again. I still remember a cold autumn day when Leonard took my new purple coat, a coat I was particularly proud of because we'd bought it in a store on the way to Momie Edna's, and held it up out of reach until I cried. I pleaded with the old preacher teacher to help me retrieve it until I heard him mutter, under his breath, "Some coat!" Though it was finally returned to me, from that day forward, I hated the coat and chose to freeze rather than wear it. Tall Leonard was never disciplined by the old preacher teacher, for that or any other incident.

In his book *The Whistling Season,* the author Ivan Doig writes about a one-room school:

> *"Out beyond the play area, there were round rims of shadow on the patch of prairie where the horses we rode to school had eaten the grass down in circles around their picket stakes.....the trails in the grass that radiated in as many directions as there were homesteads with children, all converging to that school-yard spot ...Forever and a day could go by, and that feeling will never leave me. Of knowing, in that instant, the central power of that country school in all our lives: those trails leading to the school. How their pattern held together a neighborhood!"*

If Mr. Doig was right about how a community's character can be gauged by its school, then Mother had surely moved us straight into hell. As the school year continued, I came to fear that old preacher teacher so much that I faked poison ivy outbreaks, colds and various other infirmities in order to miss school. Eventually my father took pity on me and intervened with the Board of Education in Pineville. When he explained to the school superintendent that my brother and I were both good students and how the one-room school was inadequate, we were given a special dispensation. With the express understanding that should Haford or I ever create a problem for the bus driver the privilege would be revoked, we were allowed to ride the high school bus into a nearby town and be dropped off at the elementary school en route. It was a good thing that Dad didn't take my brother along to that meeting! I always knew my father was a smart man.

We never went back to the one-room school and we were told that a few short years later, it closed entirely. As for the old preacher teacher, I hope for the sake of small children and education that he was finally put out to pasture.

I sincerely wish I could tell you that was the only bad experience I ever had with a clergyman, but I cannot.

That's another story.

OLD MAN MACK

It's not the first time she has sent us out with him by ourselves in the family car. Why didn't she go with us? Why did she stay home and let a stranger borrow the car? She has forgotten me before but she likes the car—that's why Daddy has to catch a ride to work.

I know by now what's coming, so as soon as he pushes me into the front seat to sit by him and insists that Haf get into the back, I quickly slip out the passenger-side door and hide in the bushes. I hate bugs and am terrified of snakes but I am much more afraid of "Old Man" Mack.

Now, Haford is still in the back seat waiting and Mack is outside the car looking all around and calling out for me. I know hiding is futile because he will never give up on finding me and just drive on off. After all, the only reason he manufactured the trip was to get me into the front seat of the car, in the dark with him.

He eventually gets me back into the car and pulls me close to him as the car is moving away. I'm only nine years old and don't even know yet about pubic hair. What he's doing is strange and sickening but he is a preacher, so surely, no matter how bad this feels, there must be some good reason for God to allow this to happen. I'm sure that's it—it's something he has to do and he can't help it. He's just doing God's will.

*We finally traverse the four miles of bumpy dirt road
and get out onto the two-lane pavement that takes us a short
distance further to his relatives' house. When we arrive
there and go inside, how is it possible that no one notices the
changes in me? How did I get to be so completely invisible?*

*I lie on the floor while he visits and talks about the Bible.
My brother plays nearby. I keep looking at the bubbles in
Christmas lights on the tree. The lights look like candles,
filled with colored water, set on tiny saucers. I focus on the
pretty tree lights with the many bright colors and constant
motion, and dread the end of the visit, which means another
car ride with that old man making me do disgusting things.
He won't leave until I'm sitting close to him on the front
seat. I keep asking my brother to sit up front but he won't let
that happen.*

*On one pitch black night we get out of the car and
approach the narrow walk bridge. He begins trying to hug
me again and says, "It's really your mother I want—it's
her I want to do these things to." This was taking place as
we made our way across a make-shift bridge made of two
boards nailed onto a log. It is the only thing between us and
the raging creek below.*

*I'm holding onto the wobbly handrail for dear life and,
perhaps because of the danger in this very act, I get up
enough courage to say, "I'm going to tell my daddy on you."
I then break away and run like the devil, in the freezing cold,
up the long lane that leads to the old farmhouse.*

I didn't expect my prayers to be answered—after all, I had prayed
every single night for him to go away, to die, or something. But when
I awakened the following morning, I thought I had witnessed a
miracle. "Old Man" Mack was gone!

In reality, he had awakened in the middle of the night and waited for my dad to get home from the mines. As my father told the story of the night's events, Old Man Mack had gone to sleep and had a dream—a vision, he said—that a member of his family was gravely ill. He said God was telling him to immediately return home to Kentucky and convinced Daddy to take him to a nearby town and drop him off at a bus depot where he could get a ticket back home.

I then realized there had been no miracle, that Old Man Mack had believed me when I threatened to tell. He simply wanted to be gone before I woke up the next morning!

I was so relieved and, like any nine year old child, I wanted desperately to tell someone what had happened but, even at that young age, I understood the consequences of telling. I knew I couldn't tell Daddy because he might have gone after Old Man Mack and kill him, and then be sent to jail. I knew not to tell my Mother because she would be furious with me—telling would get her in trouble with Dad. He hadn't wanted that man in our home in the first place.

During the time when Mack lived with us, he and Mother got up at the crack of dawn every day and went to Pineville to do a live Christian radio show. He had stayed at our house during a recent revival and either came back again later or simply stayed on, just to be near her… or *me*. His sister-in-law lived only a few doors from the church, within walking distance. I wondered why he didn't stay there instead of at our house. They had girls, too. Maybe they'd known about him.

That wasn't the only time I was forgotten and left unprotected while my mother chased some illusion of her own. After Mack left she started following our pastor everywhere, like a "groupie."

When I was 13 or 14, she would ride in the front passenger seat of the car while the preacher's son kissed me in the back seat. Occasionally I got concerned about being caught, until one night I realized why we were there and understood, with perfect clarity, that she would never bother me as long as I kept my mouth shut. She didn't care what I was doing in the back seat as long as she could follow her preacher around from church to church. She continued to use me as a chaperone until the gossip became more powerful than the two of them.

Mother went on to start a youth group at our church. She would pick up a truckload of kids—literally a truck load—and take them to the weekly meetings. She never seemed to have time for me but she sure was popular with the other young people. I remember all the kids would tell me how great it must be to have a mother who was so much fun.

Many years later, I discovered that I could look up names on the Social Security "Death Index" website and find out if and when and how a person had died. I also found sites that listed the locations of cemeteries and names of persons buried in them.

I knew the name of the town Old Man Mack had come from, and after a brief search, I found the location of his gravesite. (Since I can't just walk up and urinate on his grave, I'll have to settle for spitting. That business of the disadvantages of not being born male seems to keep following me around.)

I called some of his relatives on the pretense that I wanted to return some books and a Bible he had left at our home when I was a child. The in-laws who answered the phone were cordial, but none of his surviving children wanted to talk about him at all. And wasn't it odd that he had not been buried near or even in the same cemetery as his wife?

Every time I hear the quote, "We are the sum total of our experiences" it has profound and special meaning for me. When people make comments or jokes about aging, I always say that the thing I hate most about it is all the old men, especially old preachers. Everyone laughs, including me, but I know it's not really a joke.

After another failed marriage, I remember seeing the movie "Frankie and Johnnie" and, unrealistically, wishing I could meet a man who would not give up on me; one who would keep beating down the barriers and sticking by me until I came around to relaxing enough to trust again; someone like Frankie. Did I say again?

Instead, I am now married to a man who only pays attention to me if there isn't another living soul present. As soon as we were married it was like a light went out; that job was done.

All our friends say, "What a nice guy, it must be great to be married to someone who is so popular and well liked." It seems that I've married my mother after all.

Now that I've finally written about all of this, and my darkest secrets are out, it must mean that I'm done with it. Finished! I will never again feel claustrophobic in a car I'm not driving, will never again cringe whenever my husband forgets and grabs my leg just above the knee. I won't even think "hypocrite" when I hear someone talk about fasting for spiritual reasons. It's okay now.

Of course, I know better; in fact just saying that makes me laugh as I'm reminded of a clipping I once taped on my refrigerator. It goes something like this: "Thinking you can fix yourself just by admitting and facing the cause of your problems is like thinking you can eat once and be done with it." I do understand that, as with every other kind of healing in life, it's always a process.

However, each moment of facing the truth makes me a little better, a little more sane and less likely to blame others for my own conditioned reactions. I've also learned to use caution when I meet someone with whom I feel an instant connection. The attraction may very well be the manifestation of recognition.

Sentimental Journey

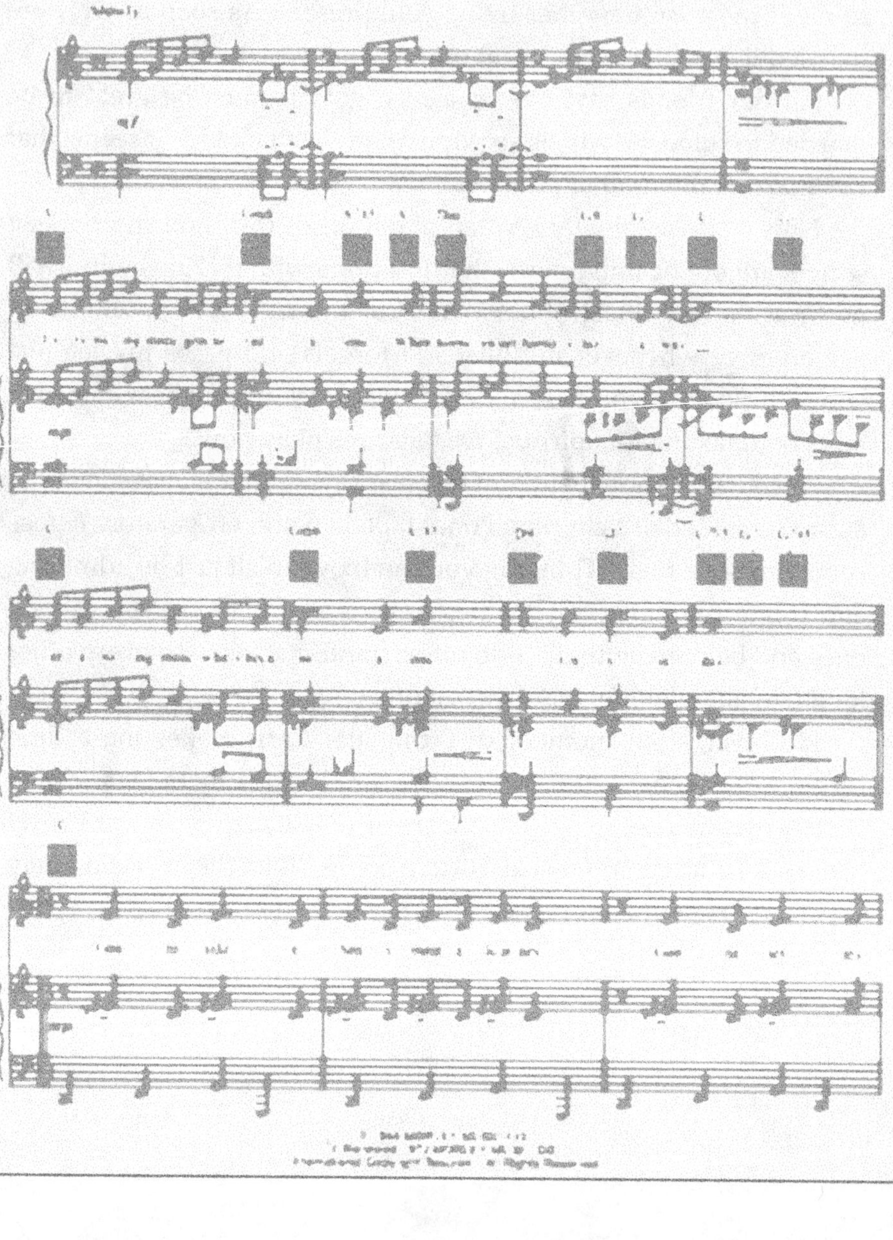

SENTIMENTAL JOURNEY

*H*ave you ever noticed how closely some memories are tied to music? How a single song can trigger an entire storied excerpt from the past?

There are many songs that serve as examples of the phenomenon for me—a few that are still current, but most of which can be heard only on "Oldies" radio stations.

My first hospital visit is powerfully linked to music. Just the other day, I heard a song that triggered a long forgotten memory to come flooding back, taking me on a sentimental journey.

When I was about seven years old, a nurse came to our school to perform annual checkups on all the students. The school, owned by the Koppers Coal Company, was one of the best in the state, and the annual physical checkups were just one of the many services provided by the company for which my father worked.

After my examination, the nurse sent a message home to my parents informing them that I had a condition known as amblyopia, or "lazy eye."

I'm certain that my parents had already noticed the problem, but because I had an aunt and other relatives with the same trait, assumed it was an inherited and, therefore, untreatable condition. Until then, I don't think they understood that I could lose sight in the eye that was weak.

Once informed, Mom and Dad took me to several doctors, including one in Ohio whom my aunt had highly recommended. We made the long trip with high hopes only to have them dashed. "We can do surgery, with some risks, to straighten the eye," they all said, "but it's too late to save the vision."

It was at that point that I first wore glasses. I'm not sure if they were prescribed because my right eye was also weak or if the vision correction was supposed to strengthen the muscles in my left eye, to keep it straight. I just knew that the glasses made me feel a little better. I could hide behind them to some extent.

I would sometimes catch my mother gazing at me with a sad expression on her face. "What a shame," she would say. "You would have been pretty if you hadn't been born cross-eyed."

I wondered at first, when she insisted on moving out of the coal camp community, if it was to hide me because she was ashamed of me and not because she wanted to live on a farm as she told her friends.

Despite the glasses, my lazy eye continued to turn inward, and the teasing of other school children, who called me "four eyes" and "that cross-eyed girl" made life miserable. I began to plead with my parents to allow me to have the surgery to straighten my eye, but they refused, explaining that they were afraid something would go wrong. They told me I would have to wait and make the decision when I was an adult, and responsible for myself.

On Saturdays after we moved to the country, my parents went shopping in town for groceries and farm supplies. I always stayed home, and would stand at the picture window and watch the car as it moved down the long drive and across the rickety wooden bridge. When they disappeared from sight, I immediately rushed to turn on the television and stare at the snowy pictures of Pentecostal preachers and their healing services. I don't recall that any scriptures were read but, after some very loud preaching, they invariably asked for money, and were sure to repeat several times the mailing address where one's check could be sent.

Toward the end of the show, the preacher prayed for all viewers with infirmities like me. We were instructed to pray along with him and to lay our hands on the television screen. I lost count of how many times I stood with my eyes tightly closed, my outstretched hands pressed against that dusty old black and white television.

Sometimes I was so convinced my eye had been healed that, as soon as the praying stopped, I raced to my room to look in the mirror. But I was always disappointed. People on the show got up from their wheelchairs and walked, smiling into the cheering congregation, but my eye was never healed. I was sure it was all because I had no money to send the preachers.

In addition to feeling ugly, I had a strange sense of imbalance. On one of our rare visits back to the coal camp, I attempted to ride my friend's bicycle. I didn't have one of my own because there was no place to ride on the bumpy dirt road in the country. My first and only bicycle ride only lasted about two minutes before I crashed into the side of a house. When I untangled my skinned legs and pulled myself up with bloody hands, I was met by Mother, who was screaming, "Why did you even try that? You know how clumsy you are!"

I hid behind my thick glasses, biding time, until I tormented my parents to the breaking point. Relenting, my father took me to the Blaydes Vision Clinic in Bluefield, West Virginia, reputed to be the best in the country.

After a thorough examination and a lengthy consultation, the doctor scheduled a date for the operation. On the appointed day I was admitted to the hospital and taken to the operating room where I was greeted by the anesthesiologist. They had explained to us that, because the surgery for amblyopia was such a delicate procedure, they would use a general anesthesia called ether. The nurse told me to count backwards from ten as the ether was started. I heard the song "Sentimental Journey." I looked around for the source and spotted a small brown radio. While listening to the music, I felt and fought the ether as it pulled me down under its overwhelming grip of suffocation. As I lost consciousness, I understood what drowning would feel like. I was 14 years old and had not yet learned to swim. I knew in that instant I never would.

The day I was originally scheduled to be released, I sat on the edge of the high hospital bed as the doctors carefully began unwrapping the bandages. My mother looked on as the drama built in a scene not unlike one from a soap opera. I remember a nurse standing by, holding a mirror in her hand. I was so terrified that I would still have a crossed eye that I fainted—passed out cold. Needless to say, the doctors decided I needed to remain in the hospital for another day.

By the time we got home, Dad was already at work in the mines, where he worked the second shift. The next morning, I opened my eyes to see my dad staring down at me. "I thought you would look a lot worse," he said, "but you look good—not at all like you've been through surgery."

The surgery was a success but, like most things in this life, it was not perfect. I stopped wearing glasses, but I learned to keep my gaze always to the left or right in a conversation. In photographs, when a flash is used, even now, my lazy eye appears. I have always hated having my picture taken.

Throughout most of my young life a feeling of insecurity and low self esteem plagued me. I couldn't seem to escape thoughts such as "take what you're offered, cross-eyed girl, because you won't be offered much." Even into adulthood, that mentality prevailed and influenced many of my life choices.

When I was in high school, a girl who rode our bus and lived even further up that dirt road "holler" had a lazy eye even more pronounced than mine had been. Thinking it might help her, I shared my story. She listened intently until I finished talking and then began to cry. "My father doesn't have a good job with insurance, like yours," she said. Several years later, I ran into Patty at a local store and noticed her eye had been straightened. We exchanged knowing smiles and went on our way.

In the early 70's, I moved with my then husband and family to a town in Turkey where only five other American families resided. I felt strangely liberated. I was, for the first time in my life, free from the people who were all too familiar with my past. Every weekend we either hosted or attended a party. I danced as if no one were watching, tasted my first adult beverage and drank enough champagne, over the next two years, to fill the immersion pool at the Baptist church I had left behind.

I had little in common with the few American women there, but I became good friends with one who told me that the thing she appreciated most about our friendship was the way we could look each other straight in the eye and tell the truth about anything. She then burst out laughing. "I guess we can't really do that, can we?"

I wasn't sure what Carolyn was implying until she pointed out that she too had a lazy eye. It was then that I was flooded with relief at the realization that I had forgotten to be self conscious. After all those years, I finally began to look people "straight in the eye" without trying to hide.

A few years ago a young man who works for me in my design business injured his eye and had to have a cornea transplant. During the time he was without vision in the eye he complained that his balance was off. A light went on in my head, and I said, "I've been legally blind in one eye since I was seven years old. Do you suppose that's why I can't dance well or ride a bicycle?"

"I can guarantee you it is," he said.

For the remainder of the day I contemplated the meaning of that enlightenment with a huge sense of relief. There was a reason for my awkwardness—it was not, after all, a commentary on my value as a person.

I still hate that damned old song, but another benefit to growing older is that "Sentimental Journey" is rarely heard anywhere these days. I was fifty years old when I took my first lesson but I did learn to swim. I don't particularly enjoy it, but I won't die by drowning—in water or self-pity. Like many, my journey has not been easy, nor has it been without mistakes. I have been wounded many times and have the scars to prove it. But I have survived with my spirit intact and I believe it always will be.

I still can't ride a bicycle. No one expects it of me and I wouldn't take the risk now of breaking these old brittle bones even if they did. But sometimes, when I'm alone at the mountain house, and think of my daughters, I turn up the music they listened to as teenagers so loud that I can feel it.

And I dance!

STRANGE & UNUSUAL EVENTS

It was a clear summer day, idyllic really, not a cloud in the sky. The gentle breeze was quiet as death. I was sitting on a rock watching my brother catch crawdads when my once cool perch started to feel warmer than when I first sat down upon it. I stood up and stared down at the stream—the water was beginning to boil. All the rocks, even the boulder-sized one I had been sitting on, were bubbling up and down like a giant pot of eggs boiling.

I began running and screamed for my brother to follow. Something awful was happening. We ran as fast as a nine-year-old girl and an eight-year-old boy could, toward home and safety but it wasn't fast enough. It became hard to see, as a torrent of multi-colored worms descended upon us. I pushed my way through with one arm but lost hold of my brother's arm. When I finally managed to get close to the house, the air began to clear but the structure was gone. Vanished! In its place was a clearing with new bright green grass.

I don't know how long I had slapped at my reddened arms or how loudly I had screamed and thrashed about in my bed before I woke enough to realize I was in the midst of a nightmare.

The setting of the first part of my dream came from an everyday scene, a place where my brother and I felt safe to play. I spent many summer afternoons sitting on a large rectangular rock watching my brother catch crawdads. I didn't want to touch the scary-looking things but watching him catch them was a fascinating pastime.

The water came from the mountains in back of our house, rushed down in a narrow stream to the base of the mountain and spread out to more than ten feet wide over rocks and wild mint as it flowed past our house on its way to merge with Craney Creek. Mother often picked the mint to use when she made tea—I didn't care much for the tea but I loved the fragrance that permeated the air. It reminded me of the Beech Nut chewing gum Daddy carried in his dinner bucket to the coal mines every night.

He worked second shift and always arrived home when we were sleeping. Every morning, the first thing I did was run to the spot where he dropped his round dinner bucket and retrieved my stick of gum.

I have no idea what the dream meant, or if it had any meaning at all, but the memory of it still haunts me. I suspect it had something to do with the stories our mother told us about hell soon after she got religion. She said if we told a lie or did anything "bad," the devil would reach up through the ground, grab us and drag us down to hell with him. That whole line of thought was certainly fodder for nightmares but they didn't stop when I grew older and was no longer afraid of the "Boogie Man."

Eight years later, when I was 17 and a senior in high school, my parents built a new smaller house next door. It was so close to the old farmhouse we had moved to that I could (and often did) crawl out a window from the old house into my new room in the unfinished one.

By the spring of the next year, we had moved and the farmhouse had been torn down. One day, as I was walking from the concrete block pump house where our washing machine was installed, I glanced at the spot where the old house had once stood. I was stunned by the scene before me—to the finest detail, including the bright green grass, it was the scene from the nightmare I'd first had almost a decade before.

Other dreams eventually came to pass—most of them dreams from my childhood but occasionally as an adult as well. I dreamed, for example, that my mother's brother would die in an automobile accident.

I had hated and feared that particular uncle for most of my life—it was rumored that on one hot August day, he had made his three-year-old daughter undress and sit on a steaming rock until her bottom was blistered. After that, my cousin Bonnie Jean and I tried to protect our young cousin when we were around, hiding her from him when he was in a bad mood. An alcoholic known to commit atrocious acts while drunk, I was sure that the alcohol had little to do with it—he was simply evil.

He came to our home in West Virginia when I was four or five years old and while he was there—I suppose out of boredom or a need to satisfy his cruel streak—he announced that he was going to teach me a "lesson." I loved ice cream and ate it every day, and he forced me to eat it until I vomited, during which he laughed hysterically. (I never understood why my mother allowed him to do that to me though, in retrospect, I suspect she was afraid of him too.)

Within weeks of my dream, he indeed was involved in a serious wreck, but refused transport to a hospital. He was taken to my grandmother's house and laid on the bed where I always slept when we visited there. My grandmother found him dead when she went in to check on him later in the evening.

The next time I went to see her, I was afraid to go into that room, but didn't want to tell her about the dream and my fears. Before I fell asleep that night, I heard his angry voice, saying, "You let me down." Even in my state of mind, I remember feeling more anger than fear. I thought that if anyone ever deserved to go to hell, he did, but I felt a sense of guilt, for my grandmother's sake.

At some point in my life, I stopped having prophetic dreams or visions. (I suspect I repressed them out of fear that I had the power to cause them to come about.) But I still have a kind of *mentalist* sensor that has served me well. An antenna goes up when I find myself in the presence of danger or someone with evil intent. When I reflect on mistakes I've made, I often find they occurred when I ignored that "knowing" warning of my intuition.

I'm not sure that I alone was given this special gift. Instead, I strongly suspect that most everyone is born with such power, a built-in capacity meant to protect us from harm. But eventually, our so-called "logic" takes over, and we abandon those innate abilities, along with other pure gifts that come with youth and innocence, and they atrophy from disuse. I've noticed, too, that, as I've grown older, I've become far less afraid of everything and everyone and almost oblivious to public opinion.

I recently read that when we get old, we don't *change*. Rather, we simply become more like ourselves. Does that mean that there's some unwritten promise of restoration and redemption, the return of our early gifts and innocence as compensation for the infirmities of old age?

I do hope so.

WAS I IN LOVE WITH HIM
OR HIS '57 CHEVY?

*W*hen I was sixteen years old, and finally allowed to go on my first car date, I fell madly in love. I thought I would just die if I didn't marry Bobby Cook. He didn't feel the same about me, but I continued to daydream about him throughout high school and long after.

Bobby lived near my friend Lena. We went to her house almost every evening where I sat on the front porch in hopes of catching a glimpse of my true love driving by in his red '57 Chevy. I thought it was really nice that my mother took me there so often until it occurred to me that she too had a crush—on Lena's father. But that is another story altogether.

Occasionally, I talked on the phone to a girl whom I knew Bobby was also dating. It was my way of keeping up with what he was doing and to check out my competition. Her name was Deanna—she was cuter than me and far more popular at school. I really liked Deanna but kept my distance because I felt threatened.

I prayed every night for God to make Bobby fall in love with me. But he didn't. In fact, he married someone else. When he did, I started dating George Hatfield, who just happened to be my brother's best friend. George was the only boy I dated of whom my mother approved—I imagine she thought that I would do about anything for Bobby but didn't like ole George enough to "misbehave."

Unfortunately, that wasn't exactly how it worked when you were Baptist, seventeen years old, and lived in the most boring part of the entire earth.

I married good ole George and we had two beautiful daughters together, but still, at times, I thought my life would have been really perfect if only I had married Bobby. Many years later, Bobby happened to be visiting in the town where we lived and, when he called to say hello, I invited him to stop by our house and meet my children. I guess I also wanted to show off just a little.

Of course, my girls were very polite, and so was I, but it was difficult to contain my surprise and extreme disappointment. I swear that boy hadn't visited a dentist since high school. I tried not to stare but I think he actually had holes in some of his teeth! He smiled in spite of it, as if he were completely unaware that smiling, for him, was a bad idea.

After he left, one of my daughters looked at me and said, "And you liked him better than Daddy?"

They were my sentiments exactly. How humiliating it was for me to realize that I had carried a torch all those wasted years for someone who was nothing more than a teenage girl's illusion!

Every time I think back to that embarrassing moment, I hear the lyrics from a Garth Brooks song: "Some of God's greatest gifts are unanswered prayers." Do I *ever* thank God for saving me from *that* fate!

Some years ago, Deanna and I found each other again through email exchanges between some of our old high school class mates. Now very close friends, I visit her in Alabama and we'll sit around talking at night over a glass of wine. We'll wonder aloud what happened to "what's-his-name." But that's as far as it will go.

Neither of us cares enough to actually go to the trouble to find out.

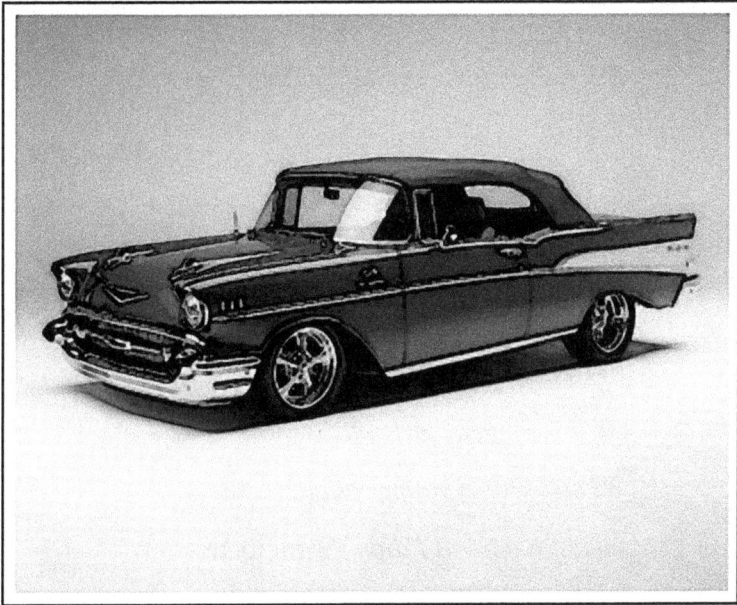

A DIFFERENT MOTHER

by Nadine Justice

What does the name "mother" mean?

Not the same for everyone;

it should, but it doesn't.

For me, it kept changing.

At age five, it meant home,

At age ten, neglect and fear.

As a teenaged girl—mistrust.

When I was a young adult, it

meant a person I didn't want to be.

In my middle years, it meant forgiveness.

Now, as I approach her age, it means home.

NELL RUTH

She was pretty and well-groomed, yet she looked more at ease with a garden hoe in her hands. She swore like a sailor, yet was a religious fanatic. She was a great mother, and an abusive one. She was a teetotaler, yet made and drank wonderful wine. She loved her husband but was an unfaithful wife. She adhered to all the strict rules of her church; she drank whiskey and danced every night in a different sleazy club. Her name was Nell Ruth. And she was my mother.

When I was a little girl and we lived in the coal camp community, my mother was nothing like the woman she later became. In my memories of that time, she is wearing a pretty white and black-striped dress and high heeled shoes, and her nails are painted red. I don't remember her yelling at us and certainly never heard her cursing my brother and me.

I would wonder later if that was because she was conscious of—and catering to—the opinions and judgment of our closest neighbors because when we moved to the "holler," no one could hear her and there were no neighbors to see her. After that, she rarely dressed up or wore make-up, and I never saw her with manicured nails again.

There were many nights when she shook me awake, sobbing apologies. "I'm a horrible mother," she would say. "Please forgive me. I'll never hit you again. Are you all right?"

I just wanted to be left alone to sleep because I knew it would probably happen again the very next night, and it often did. She was nervous the whole first year after we moved to the abandoned farmhouse. She would fly into a rage, screaming and calling Haford and me awful names, eventually hitting one or both of us with whatever she could find—usually a belt. The next evening she might make fudge and happily play "Monopoly" with us. I thought she had lost her mind. I was sure she had ruined my life.

I remember being appalled by what I considered her awful decorating tactics. Mom glued and /or nailed rolled linoleum intended for flooring onto the drafty, cracked walls and painted it a blue-green color often used for the exteriors of Federal style homes. She used the same vinyl material to cover the floors.

The base color of the linoleum came in white or gray. She painted the rugs and then, using plastic pot scrubbers, spattered three or four bright colors onto the surface. The effect was so well-received by her friends that many of them copied her design. As I look back today on the way she transformed that old house, I am no longer critical. It only recently occurred to me that I might have inherited some talent from her.

During the days when Mom was busy making the house livable, we helped, and, at times, enjoyed a hopeful sense of peace. On other days, she screamed orders and called us names, telling us how stupid we were when our feeble attempts fell short of her expectations.

This up and down drama was our normal home life until one Saturday night, when she decided to go to a tent revival. That event was going to change the course of her life—and that of her children's lives as well.

For several months afterwards, our home felt like a safe place. Then she became fanatically involved in her religion and forgot her children. At least she forgot me.

Even so, my mother shaped my attitudes toward men, religion, self confidence (or the lack of it), and most everything else in my life.

In fact, she had so much power over me that when my brother was on the brink of death after surgery for a ruptured appendix, I found myself praying to her and God simultaneously—eight months after she died!

I feared her and never came to trust her, yet I believe now that she loved her children, including me. I'm not exactly sure when I came to understand that Mother was helpless and therefore not wholly to blame. Even after that realization, I didn't immediately take responsibility for my own healing, and delayed the process as a result.

If I could do it over, I would get to the point of releasing the two of us more quickly. I imagine that she would have been relieved and I would have been free much earlier than we were. I regret not knowing I could have easily given us both that gift—a truth that came to me late in her life. If I had, I would be able to think of her now without climbing over and past the hurt look in her eyes from my unkind words. How I wish for that.

I had the power to forgive my mother all along, and though the knowledge was long in coming, I have forgiven her. It didn't happen because she died—but because now, as I approach the age she was when she died, I have lived my own imperfect life long enough to have learned the real meaning of forgiveness.

REDESIGNING A MOTHER AND DAUGHTER RELATIONSHIP

For several years after Dad died, Mother had a high old time making wine and dancing. She turned out some of the most potent and best tasting wine I've ever had and I think that woman danced in every sleazy night club in Kentucky. Anytime I traveled to Kentucky to visit her for a weekend, it would take two days for me to rest up afterwards.

I remember once when she took me dancing with her and, as the band began playing one of my favorite songs, I looked up to see a nice looking young man walking in our direction. Naturally, I assumed he was coming over to ask me to dance. Wrong! Apparently he had danced with Mother before and knew she was a good dancer. I was not, and he didn't even look at me. On one long weekend, when my older daughter Sherrie was still at Marshall University in Huntington, she and a girlfriend decided to visit Mother since she lived only a two- or three-hour drive away. On Sunday night, when all the other girls were back in the dorms exchanging stories about how they had spent their weekends, they noticed that these two girls also complained about being exhausted.

One of them said, "Wait a minute. I thought you two went to visit Sherrie's *grandmother*. Why are you so tired?"

The friend grinned. "We did but, obviously, you haven't met *Sherrie's* grandmother."

She may not have been my idea of a good mother but she sure was a fun grandmother for my two daughters. In fact, all the grandchildren loved going to her house. She was a hypochondriac who took a pill if she sneezed and she had a habit of saying "I'm so bad off I can't hardly hold my head up. I just have to take a nap." If anyone then started getting ready to go shopping, or to go anywhere for any reason, mother would pop up off the couch saying, "Let me pee and get my pocket book and I'll go with you." That line is still a favorite joke in the family, especially among Mother's grandchildren.

When Mother finally slowed down, she decided that the house, and the many acres of beautiful land with the rolling hills she so enjoyed, would soon be too much to take care of by herself. So, when she sold it and moved into town, we were all, especially Mother herself, concerned that she would be unhappy and filled with regret. With some trepidation, I called on the night of her big move to see how she was doing. "Lord, have mercy, Honey," she said, "I wouldn't trade that whole farm for this Jacuzzi. I wish I had done this years ago. The only problem is that not a single piece of my furniture will fit in this house."

I was happy to hear it. This was a problem I could do something about. "Mother, wait until I can arrange to take a few days off work and I'll come up and fix that for you," I told her. "In the meantime, please send me a copy of your new home's floor plan and don't get rid of anything until I get there."

For the next few weeks I began collecting accessories and drawing floor plans. I spent every spare moment sewing, often working well past midnight. I made window treatments, decorative pillows plus a table skirt with a coordinating topper, trimmed with fringe and complete with matching tassels on the corners. I hate to sew, but I was thankful I had learned how during my design training.

When that long weekend finally came, I headed up to Kentucky with my little red car packed so high and full there wasn't a square inch of empty space left. I had to rely on the side mirrors when passing other cars because all I could see in my rear view mirror were lamps, pictures, mirrors, wall brackets, my tool kit, and the infamous custom work—the products of my sewing skills.

I had made arrangements in advance for my three siblings, who lived near Mother, to meet me at her house, and had asked her to plan a shopping trip or a visit with a friend while we worked our magic. I explained that this was "standard protocol" for designers and that it was easier for me to concentrate if the homeowner was away.

Of course, the queen of control didn't like it, but she agreed. (I used to tell her that I couldn't walk across a room without her telling me how many steps to take.) With this background knowledge of her, I knew that asking her to leave while we rearranged her house was asking for a lot. I also knew that there would be no way to accomplish the job if she stuck around and interfered at every turn. Whenever it's necessary to chastise myself for my own controlling nature, I lighten up with a smile, I know where I got it from.

I felt sorry for the grandson who was to accompany her on the shopping trip and could only imagine how much "fun" it was going to be for him, as I watched them leave. She was wearing an angry look that said she was mad as a hornet about being caught in a web conceived by one of her own children, rendering her helpless. She always hated having anyone mess with her stuff in her absence.

As it happened, my brother Shawn had extensive experience with drapery installation, and my other brother, Haford, could do most anything. My little sister Teresa brought food and also pitched in to help with the work. This assembled crew, made up of Nell Ruth's children, sprang into action like a well-oiled machine even before Mother had exited the driveway.

In a few hours we had moved and rearranged all of the furniture, hung the pictures and mirrors, installed draperies, and placed accessories. We were able to use every item of furniture she owned, as well as all the things I had brought.

When everything was in place and we were ready for the big "reveal," Mother walked through the back door not a minute later than the agreed-upon time for her return. She entered wearing the same angry look, her grandson trailing behind looking equally apprehensive.

However, as she continued in from the garage, through the kitchen, and finally on to the dining area, "the look" slowly began to dissipate. With each advancing step, her face softened a little more. With a big sigh of relief, she said, "I was afraid I wasn't going to like it, but I never dreamed my house could look this good!"

After my brothers and sister left for their respective homes, Mother and I continued to unpack pictures and other favorite things as we moved the decorating project on into the bedrooms. We were like a couple of children who had discovered a new game. She was so exited that, before I could finish hanging a picture or placing an accessory, she would come running in the room, holding up another one of her freshly unpacked treasures, saying something like, "I know this probably won't work but Momie gave it to me and I've always loved it. So, if you can use it somewhere that would be great. But if not, that's okay too." Invariably I found the perfect spot for whatever item she presented.

While we were still working, Mother's sister, my aunt Eunice, called. I overheard Mother say, "I can't wait for you to come see my new house. You're not going to believe it. Nadine is here decorating it and boy, does she know her onions." I never did figure out how, or from where that colloquialism came, but I had no doubt about it's meaning. I had my mother's approval—even her admiration. It was all I had ever wanted!

Every night, these two widowed sisters would wait until one minute after eleven o'clock (when the long distance rates were lower) and talk until midnight. However, on this particular night, the ritual was preempted because Mother was so eager to get back to our decorating project that she managed to get off the phone in record time. We unpacked and placed things until at least two o'clock in the morning, went to bed for a few hours, and then got up the next morning and started up again. When we were both satisfied with the results of our work, I got ready for my return trip home and we drove separate cars to Lexington so that I could advise her on the window blinds that still needed to be ordered.

I can still picture my mother's face and how pretty and sweet she looked, in spite of a twinge of concern, as she gave our sales person the order information. I knew that, even as happy and excited as she was with all her new things, the strain of the expense on her limited budget took away some of the fun. It made me sad that I wasn't able to buy the blinds for her.

It was so late when I finally got on the road for the seven-hour drive back to Atlanta that I didn't arrive home until well after midnight, and I had to work the next day. I never told her about the speeding ticket I got on the way home that night.

Helping Mother decorate her new house was a turning point toward a new relationship. The experience enabled me to forgive her and, as a result, gave her great relief because she understood. She knew that I loved her and that the opportunity for me to give her the gift of my hard work, the benefit of my training, and a talent God had blessed me with, was no small occasion. And I had the comfort of knowing that I had finally made peace with her and myself.

I had no way of knowing then that it would be less than two years later that I would find myself standing in the greeting card aisle of a Hallmark store crying because out of habit, I had come there to select a Mother's Day card for someone no longer around to receive it. My mother contracted pneumonia and died unexpectedly, when she was barely 70 years old.

I returned the card to the slot and went for a long walk. I couldn't believe how much I missed her. Thankfully, I learned, while I could still tell her myself, that the love for one's parent is not dependent on perfection.

I still miss her. I will always miss her.

THE DAY WE SANG MOTHER HOME

It is February 1995. I can still see myself sitting, silent, in a dark room outside the ICU nurses' station in a hospital in Lexington, Kentucky. It is 5:00 o'clock in the morning. My family members have all gone—they are going to church today to pray for a miracle. A miracle is happening but they don't see it because it doesn't look like one—at least not the miracle we want.

I am dressed in my best suit because what I must do calls for my best everything. I'm afraid but strong. I feel like I imagine Jesus must have felt in the garden of Gethsemane—I wish this bitter cup could pass from me but I know I am the one who must do this painful thing.

I sit, numbed, and wait. I expect the doctor will be making her rounds anytime now. Last night, a nurse came into mother's room and found me standing, just looking at her. No matter how I had prayed for some other answer, I knew the decision had already been made.

The nurse approached me to ask why I was there and how I had gotten into an ICU room at 2:00 a.m. I said, "She is my mother and I want to allow her to go." The nurse responded, "You are right. If ever I saw anyone who was ready, this little lady is." She remarked that she had told Mother's doctor to let her go as well.

I knew my meeting with Dr. George would not go well. All the other doctors were in agreement that Mother's chance of survival was maybe ten percent, and her quality of life would be miserable if she survived at all. I knew that Dr. George was Mother's friend and was probably not accepting the fact that all her own efforts to save her friend and patient were failing.

Mother had been admitted to the ICU about two weeks earlier with pneumonia and put on a ventilator a few days later. When she had entered the hospital, she made my sister promise that no life support system of any sort would be utilized.

When Dr. George finally came into the waiting room to see me she was already alerted by the night nurse as to what my request would be. She did not agree but said she would ask for another doctor, who was also an ethicist, to consult with me and my family members.

The following evening the other doctor met with us and very gently and thoroughly explained the procedure. He cautioned that we should most carefully consider the aftermath and the effect the decision would have on our own psyche forever. We understood their concern—Mother was still mentally alert.

The next morning, on February 28, 1995 at 9:00 a.m., we all gathered around Mother's bed to help her on her journey from this life into the next. My sister and I held her hand and each other's as we took turns reading her favorite Bible scriptures and praying aloud for her. My brother Shawn sang the song "Wayfaring Stranger," And then we all sang "Amazing Grace." The doctors, our other relatives, Mother's minister and the nurses were all crying but we did not cry. (I will never forget seeing the doctor who was the ethicist, standing in the doorway with tears streaming down his face).

We sang beautifully together, in perfect harmony. At one point during the process, which took less than an hour, my baby sister leaned over and said, "Nadine, I didn't know you could sing."

I said, "I didn't know I could either."

Occasionally, I would lean in close to our mother's ear and whisper, "Mama, you're almost home, you're almost home, Mama," and finally, peacefully, she arrived there. She had just turned 70 in January.

We left the room to allow my younger sister time alone with Mother, then the family gathered in the hospital conference room to make the arrangements for her service. We selected the pallbearers, which included my former husband, George Hatfield. The funeral home, which had also taken my father 18 years earlier, was called to come for her body. Afterwards, my sister and I went to Mother's house to select the clothing she would be buried in and then we all proceeded to carry out her final wishes, which she had carefully pre-organized just eight months earlier. Her specific instructions included every detail right down to the flowers she wanted—yellow roses, which were her favorite.

Later that evening, my niece from Nebraska, my two brothers, my sister and I all gathered at Mother's home, where I was staying. We ate a nice dinner, which neighbors had brought to us. We played and sang along to gospel music on the CD player—all the old tunes she'd once sung in church and around the house–My brother and sister-in-law danced to "Will the Circle Be Unbroken?"

A few weeks later, when the house was sold, the four of us siblings met, along with my uncle—who was the executor for my mother's will, to pack and move her belongings. We each purchased the items we wanted for a price that had been determined earlier by an appraiser. These monies were then divided equally among the four of us.

We began this entire process with a prayer by my uncle Homer. Each time we encountered an item that was of obvious importance to a particular sibling, the other three would invariably say, "You take that. You should have it."

Mother's favorite hobby was playing cards, so when we came across an item that was "personal" and up for grabs, we drew from a deck of cards. (The one drawing the highest card won the item in question.) Sometimes we laughed, sometimes we cried, mostly we shared memories.

In all my years, I had never been more acutely aware of my wonderful heritage. With all its flaws and imperfections, the core values we had been taught still shined through. The love, respect, kindness, harmony and genuine class demonstrated by two brothers and two sisters was no accident—it was the gift our parents gave to us. The loving way we treat each other is the gift we keep giving to them. I am comforted by the peace of believing that we will be together for eternity. I know, because Momie Edna told me so.

SIBLINGS

*M*ost people have them and most people love them—some even like them—but the loyalty and level of solidarity between my siblings, especially during a family crisis, is a rare thing to behold. We tease each other and have disagreements like all siblings, but anyone who might make the mistake of hurting one of us would rue the day.

Memories of events during our growing up years don't always match and, partly because of our age differences, things that are important to one of us aren't remembered at all by another. In many other ways it appears we have nothing in common until we all get together. For instance, Teresa describes life in the "holler" as growing up in paradise and I tell people I grew up in hell. We're talking about the same place.

As of this writing, all four of us are healthy and happy. We all still work and have family obligations which make it impossible to get together often, especially true for me since I'm the only one who does not live in Kentucky.

Haford was born one week before my first birthday. It's no wonder Mother was in a bad mood—she had two babies when she was only 18! Sometimes, I think of us as twins—in some cultures they would call us "Irish twins." Once, when we were probably four and five years old, still living in the coal camp, one of us (probably me) started a rock fight with the Hamilton kids. I convinced Tommy's sisters to help me fill up my cardboard Quaker oatmeal box for their brother, telling them he was my "sweetheart," and then promptly delivered it to my brother instead.

Those days before we moved out of the coal camp were my favorite memories. When I think of the camp, I can almost smell the aroma of honeysuckle that drifted into our house on warm summer days from the hillside in front, and see my brother and me looking for May Apple and Jack-in-the-Pulpit. After we moved to Clear Fork "holler" and eventually rode the bus into Oceana for school I never worried about being picked on because I knew my "brudder" would take care of that.

Shawn came along when I was eight years old. Six months later we moved from the coal camp. Somehow I thought the move was his fault. It was a cold March day when we moved into that old and drafty farmhouse. Long abandoned, the house had no indoor plumbing, and the room that would become my bedroom had cracks in the floor wide enough that I could watch the chickens playing in the dirt underneath. I couldn't help feeling jealous because mother focused all her attention on my little brother, whom we called "Shawny Boy." (The family joked that if the temperature dropped below 50 degrees, she carried him around with a blanket thrown over his head, hence the nickname by which we call him to this day.)

There must been something magic in that blanket she draped over him because now he is the sweetest brother anyone could ever have and the kindest man I know. It was much later in life that it occurred to me her anxiety about Shawn's health may have been because it was only three years before Shawn was born that she'd lost my angel brothers.

Haford seemed happy living in the country. He got a pony and Daddy taught him to drive the truck and tractor. I hated the place and was teased mercilessly because I rarely ventured off the porch. I hated getting dirty and I was terrified of snakes—and they were plentiful.

Over time, I became more and more a recluse, staying in my room for days on end. I imagined, when I wasn't in school, that a small plane had crashed in a nearby field, that my "real" parents were dead and that these people were at least kind enough to give me a place to stay until my relatives from the city were located. I waited every day for them to come and rescue me—that fantasy was my salvation.

Mother seemed to be completely unaware of my loneliness, but since there was no one else for her to talk to, she began treating me as a confidante and telling me things that were inappropriate for children my age to hear. That made me so uncomfortable that by the time I was a teenager, I had retreated even further.

Then, when I was seventeen, Mother called me in for a "sit-down" talk. She looked nervous. "I'm pregnant," she said. I'll never forget the relief on her pretty face when she saw how excited I was about her news. We could make baby clothes and shop together and maybe she could crochet some things like she used to make for my dolls when I was little. I was full of ideas. It had been a very long time since I had felt close to my mother. We had something to look forward to and it was one of the few happy times during my teenage years.

Mother was so concerned that I would be embarrassed about my 34- and 50-year-old parents having a baby that, as compensation, she agreed to let me name the new sibling, a decision she would later regret. And I'm sure my sister has never forgiven me for naming her Teresa LaVerne. (I do have a perfectly legitimate explanation but that's a story for another time.)

I don't recall the name I had in mind if she had been a boy. Probably the name of my then current boyfriend. (I don't recall that either.) However, I do clearly remember being awakened by my mother in the middle of a snowy night in early December.

I had made her promise to let me go with her to the hospital when the time came. Dad had already started the car to get it warm and Mother was calmly getting ready to go. I panicked. What if they got stuck in the snow storm en route to the hospital, which was nearly two hours away? What would we do? I didn't know nothin' 'bout birthin' no babies!

Not willing to admit that I had chickened out, I offered up my concern for Shawn and Haford, who *certainly* couldn't be left alone, I said. So, I reasoned, I might be more help staying home and taking care of them. I'm sure my story didn't hold water because Haford was only one year younger than I was and perfectly capable of taking care of our younger brother, Shawn. And my brothers would have eaten worms before sampling my cooking. But they pretended to believe me.

With a hurried promise to call as soon as the baby arrived, they said goodbye. I watched my parents drive away into an awful snow storm, feeling more than a little guilty. I remember that I didn't sleep a wink that night but when morning came, all was well—Dad called to say we had a new baby sister.

When Teresa was about 18 months old, I left West Virginia to take a job with the telephone company in Washington, DC. I loved living in the city and loved my job but missed my family—especially my baby sister. In fact, I missed her so much that I once spent most of my paycheck on dresses for her and had to eat baked potatoes at every meal for a week. To this day, I hate baked potatoes.

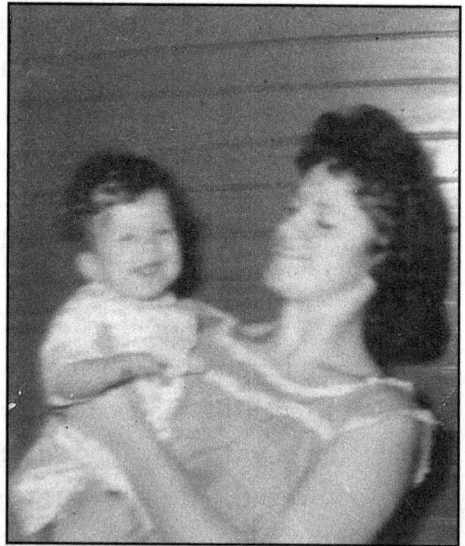

If any one of us is sick or in trouble, the other three come to the rescue. Haford once spent three weeks in a coma and Shawn, Teresa and I took turns sleeping in the hospital ICU waiting room until he was out of danger and recovering.

When the four of us get together, we joke about the colloquialisms we learned from our parents. We could probably communicate in our own secret language. In honor of that, every Christmas we manage to get together and celebrate with what we call a "Nell Ruth" style party. Anytime we venture out together to go shopping at least one of us will yell out, "Let me pee and get my pocketbook and I'll go with you!"

Mother was especially fond of mourning doves and yellow roses. Every year on her birthday and on the anniversary of her death, Teresa and I wear a yellow rose. Shortly after she passed away, we all compared stories about unusual encounters with mourning doves. I suspect to this day we each think of her, and each other, when we hear them coo.

As a result, both roses and doves are special to me. It is not an accident that my company logo is made up of a dove and two roses.

Zonguldak—overlooking the Black Sea

ZONGULDAK

Forever and a day will come and go before I forget the feeling I had that long ago day as I stood gazing out on the sea from a remote swatch of land halfway between Amasra and Zonguldak, Turkey.

When I abruptly, and without explanation, asked the driver to stop the car, I had been looking around with curiosity in much the same way as would be expected of any tourist in a new and foreign place. As we rounded a curve on the winding road, which followed the rocky coastline of the Black Sea, I was suddenly struck by a powerful sense of recognition—a familiarity. It was as if I had been in this place before. I got out of the car and walked around half expecting to find remnants of a past life. That explanation was only a little less believable than the set of unlikely circumstances which had brought me to this strange land.

Prior to moving to Turkey I had followed my husband from what seemed like every small and dirty coal-mining town between Pennsylvania and Illinois. He worked for a company, based in Chicago, which built coal cleaning and processing plants in America as well as in a few foreign countries.

During the first five years of our marriage we moved more than twenty times. It was not uncommon for us to learn, on a Friday afternoon, that we were expected to be in another town, at least a day's drive away, by the following Monday morning. As soon as George got word from the home office, he called me and I would begin packing our meager possessions. Occasionally the transfer was postponed, which meant that I had to unpack everything and start all over again in another week or two. Even so, when my husband arrived home from work on "moving day," I was always packed, had our baby fed and dressed in her pajamas, and I was ready to drive.

Too poor to stop and get a motel room, we were always on a deadline tighter even than our budget. George would sleep while I drove through the night. I supposed that he thought, because he had worked all day and I had "nothing else to do," that that arrangement was fair. In any case, that's just the way it was.

Eventually we were transferred to Beckley, West Virginia. According to plan, so that we would not have to move again, George had taken a position with a client company there when construction of a coal preparation plant was completed.

I was more than tired of moving and longed to have another baby and a house of our own. Beckley was a small and lovely mountain-top town—an ideal place to raise a family. It was exactly what I had hoped for, partly because my parents lived only an hour away. We soon found the perfect house and two years later had the perfect baby, another beautiful girl. I was ecstatically happy as I went about decorating our wonderful new home and taking care of the children.

Everything seemed to be going well and life was good—for me. Unfortunately, George was very unhappy with his new job and as his discontent escalated, so did our arguments. He had also started to fall back into old habits of stopping in at some local watering hole before coming home from work. There were many nights when he didn't show up for dinner at all, leaving me to feed the girls and put them to bed without him.

By the time Sherrie and Sandi were two and nine years old, respectively, the complaints from their father and nights alone became almost as unbearable for me as moving every few months had been. After carefully considering alternatives, I suggested that he should contact his old company and ask if he could come back. "Of course," I said, "we can't travel with you, except maybe during summers, but we'll do the best we can and we'll manage, somehow, to have a better family life."

It must have been exactly what he had been waiting to hear because he immediately started making efforts to contact the powers-that-were at his old company, Roberts and Shaffer Construction.

Several weeks later George came home from work — on time — and announced that R & S did, in fact, have a place for him. However, he said, accepting it was out of the question because the only positions available were in either Turkey or India.

"You mean we would have to move out of the country?" I asked.

"Yes, "He replied, "and they will only accept men with families. No single men."

I'm sure he was surprised by my response. "Don't tell them 'no' just yet. Let's think about it for awhile."

I reasoned that it was a temporary project — two years at the most — and in 1971, nothing exciting was happening in Beckley, West Virginia. The country of Turkey really intrigued me. I could not resist the temptation of what I considered a possible great adventure. The pay was great and promises from the company of domestic help and additional travel were powerful incentives as well.

The only thing holding me back was the fact that my father was very ill. The doctors hadn't arrived at a diagnosis yet, and I was afraid that he might die while I was away. When he realized that I was thinking of turning it down because of him, he said, "Don't you dare miss this opportunity; I would go myself if I had the chance. You go and tell me all about it when you come back."

We then wrote a letter to the people we were to replace to get their advice and to learn more about the country of Turkey. But by the time we received an answer, we were too far down the road to be objective. It is unlikely that we could have been dissuaded by any negative information they offered. In retrospect, they presented several "cons," but also had many positive things to say. They were even kind enough to send a list of items we should bring.

The "big bosses" from Chicago took us out to dinner and interviewed me privately to determine if this move was something I could handle. It was their philosophy that an employee would not do well if his family was unhappy. I guess we passed the test, because we accepted the job. The next few months were filled with excitement and activity as we began preparing to leave our home for the eighteen months in Turkey.

As a part of the deal, en route to Turkey, we were promised an expenses-paid four-day tour to any country of our choice. Thinking that an English speaking country would be more manageable for us and our children on our first trip abroad, we opted for London, and the company allowed us to hire a private tour guide so that we could cover more points of interest in a shorter time.

One of the day tours we took was to see the changing of the guards at Buckingham Palace. We had hoped to get a glimpse of the queen and were disappointed to learn that she was out of town. But we did have a great time visiting Piccadilly Square, Madame Trousseau's Wax Museum and many other interesting sites.

On the last day of our London tour, George got a call from the home office telling him that we could either stay a few more days there or move on to another city for a brief visit. Our house in Zonguldak wasn't ready, they said, and a little more time was needed

Of course, we decided to go to another city and headed for Paris, France. We discovered that the French weren't quite as friendly as the Brits and that their traffic was frightful, but we managed to take in a few highlights and did a little shopping at the Galleries Lafayette as well.

On the following Monday, we boarded a plane to Istanbul for our connecting flight to Ankara, where the job manager and his wife, Hank and Ella Borkowsky, were waiting for us. Upon our arrival, they told us our house was still not ready but they had made arrangements for us to spend five days at the Grand Ankara Hotel. During our stay in Ankara, there was a parade to honor and welcome a special visitor. We walked outside to watch and were delighted to see that we hadn't missed seeing the queen of England at all. Instead, we saw her very up close, as her car passed just a few feet away from the entrance to our hotel.

We had a wonderful time touring the old city and visiting the sites in Ankara while they were stalling for time. But on the morning of our departure for Zonguldak, a sense of uneasiness rose to the surface and wormed its way into my mind. At that moment, I wanted to say, "Thank you for the trips to London and Paris, but I was just kidding about living in Turkey." I sensed that we were in for a huge dose of reality at the other end of our long drive.

It was a cold rainy day and nothing in Turkey looks good on cold rainy days. It was mid October and the monsoons were about to start. The company sent one driver for us and a second car for our many pieces of luggage. Hank and Ella were in yet another car, so our caravan of three cars set out for Zonguldak.

About 4½ hours into the trip, I began thinking we should be nearing our destination. Each time we approached a new little village, I would look around and think to myself, "Please, God, don't let this be Zonguldak," and breathe a sigh of relief when we passed on through. Finally, there would be no sigh.

We had been told that the population of Zonguldak was 75 thousand. As I looked around, I wondered where they were all hiding. When I observed a lone traffic light on the main street, rising feelings of panic were replaced by efforts to refrain from laughing out loud. Apparently, it had been installed for decoration only. Not a single driver stopped or even seemed to take notice; they all, including our driver, just drove on through as if it wasn't even there.

From there, we were taken to a duplex, which was to be our home for the next eighteen months. When we arrived, the Wasko family, who lived on the other side of the duplex, came over to welcome us and to explain to the Borkowskys why it was that the central heat was still not installed in our side of the house. It soon became obvious that the Waskos and Borkowskys were in a major feud and we were the pawns. Though it had been Walt Wasko's assignment to finish getting our house ready, he had done exactly the opposite to make the Borkowskys look bad. But we would be the ones who suffered.

The place was cold and damp and the only heating available were two inadequate, poorly-placed electric space heaters. The moment we were alone, George voiced exactly what I was thinking. "How could I have brought my family to this awful place?" I'm sure we all broke down into tears.

George promised to call the home office in Chicago the next morning and ask them to arrange to get us back home as quickly as possible, but I refused. "No," I said, "we're not giving up that easily. Let's agree to stick it out for six weeks and if we still hate it here, then we'll leave."

We went into a room with two twin beds that were intended for the girls, and pushed them together. We put all the covers we could find on our make-shift king-sized bed and the four of us slept that night in the same bed. Even the sheets were cold and damp, but we kept each other warm.

When we awakened the next day, the rain had stopped and the sun was shining. I opened the kitchen door and stepped out onto a tiny balcony. Just a few feet away stood a handsome Turkish man on his equally small balcony, drinking a cup of coffee. He nodded to me and in perfect English, said "Good morning. Welcome."

I had never heard more beautiful words. I replied with a hearty "thank you" and said a silent prayer. "Thank you God. Maybe this is going to be all right after all."

It was more than all right. That first morning greeting from my neighbor was a preview of the many kindnesses that were to come from these wonderful people who welcomed us and treated us as their guests. Soon our little house was filled with all the necessary comforts that make a home—music and friends and laughter. (The installation of a western style bathroom didn't hurt either.)

Each day was better than the day before. I set up a schedule for home schooling my nine-year-old and a couple of our new friends pitched in to help. To this day, I believe the result was far better than anything she might have learned in any ordinary classroom.

It still makes me sad today that many people in my country have only negative opinions of Muslims. To assume that all Muslim people are radical bomb-toting lunatics would be like expecting me, because I grew up in the hills of West Virginia, to head out for church on Sunday mornings with my own personal basket of venomous snakes. Stupidity is an affliction. Ignorance is a choice. Neither, unfortunately, is unique to a particular race, religion or country.

We celebrated their holidays and they celebrated ours, and we learned from each other. One of my favorite Christmas memories is of when our friend Muharrem, after too much wine, fell backwards into our Christmas tree and stood up—with a little help—with foil icicles dripping from his ears.

Thanksgiving was an equally fun time. Halloween, on the other hand, was a bit more difficult to explain.

I made many friends and learned enough of the language to get by. I learned creative new ways to cook, using seasonal food—olive oil, white cheese and fish.

It was a very exciting time but not all of it was easy. There were many times when the isolation of being so far from family and friends, and the impossibility of deep communication without benefit of fluency in the Turkish language was overwhelming.

But isolation can also be a great friend. The rare benefit of being removed artificially from my "real life" allowed me to take the position of observer, of being able to sort out what was authentic and what was not, to separate fake friends from genuine. I moved them about in my mind like chess pieces with clarity that otherwise might never have been available to me. I vowed to make any and all changes necessary for living a more honest and truthful life. And as soon as I returned home I did exactly that.

That long ago moment when I stood on a remote spot by the Black Sea was the clearing of a palette; a starting point for a real and genuine life. It was a singly profound moment, an instant when I knew I would never again allow myself to get caught up in the prison of fear of the expectations and opinions of others.

It was not, as I thought then, the place of another lifetime. It was the place where I would find my life.

POSTSCRIPT: As parents we can't always be sure, even after our children are grown, of how they perceive our parenting of them. When my daughters' father and I decided to move our family to another country, the only encouragement we received at the time came from *my* father. Almost everyone else thought we had lost our minds and that we surely couldn't be doing the best thing for our young children.

We, on the other hand, believed we were, and later when they both turned out to be such fine young women, we were sure of it. Both Sandi and Sherrie participated in European study tours during college. I was convinced that our early travels and exposure to other cultures broadened their minds and educations and gave them courage to do that and other things they might have otherwise missed.

Even so, the following letter was welcome confirmation:

Dear George and Nadine,

I seem to remember hearing that your friends thought you were crazy for taking your kids and moving halfway around the world. Well, crazy or not, I am grateful that you did. How many children have the opportunity at an impressionable age to see the changing of the guards at Buckingham Palace, the Eiffel Tower, the Vatican, the Church of the Nativity in Bethlehem, Venice, and to ride a camel around the Pyramids of Giza? Not many is my guess.

I vaguely remember being told about the adventure on which our family was to embark. I must have been born with an interest in different cultures and ways of life. I do remember being excited!

I had a monthly subscription in a book club of some kind. Anyway, each month I would receive in the mail a book and pictures of a different country along with a plastic record telling me of that country's cultures and traditions. I also remember asking to visit whatever the most recent issue featured.

Unfortunately, at the time, the country was communist and it would have been difficult or impossible to visit. It didn't matter, it would be an adventure and an exciting one. I suppose I may have been reluctant to leave my friends and school but I have no memory of that.

I still vividly remember the first taxi ride in London, the old city in Ankara, and the dirt road as we first approached Zonguldak. I remember the Turkish people being very welcoming and the house being quite cold. We settled in and became acclimated to our new surroundings and way of life.

I truly believe that the experience of living in Turkey shaped the person I am. I was exposed to different people, different cultures, different traditions, and a different way of life. I learned that as different as people can be, there are still many similarities. I learned to accept the differences and appreciate them. When others comment about a difference they may find odd, I hear myself reply, "Everyone is different. That is a good thing. Think how boring it would be if we were all the same." I think I am a very accepting person and that is a quality I like about myself.

While I am still not a fan of homeschooling, the education that came with the experience of living in Turkey and our travels is unparalleled and irreplaceable. I would not trade it for anything!

I've often told friends and acquaintances about what a wonderful experience I had as a child, and I realized that I haven't told you. So, thank you, thank you, thank you for uprooting me and moving me halfway around the world! I have always been and will always be grateful.

I LOVE YOU!!!!
Sherrie

DIVORCE

*W*hen my father died, I remember thinking it was the worst thing that would happen in my life. I soon discovered I was wrong—the worst thing is a demon called divorce.

Even now, whenever I hear someone say that they're getting divorced I feel like crying for my own remembered pain and for theirs yet to come. I want to scream at them "Wait, stop, you have no idea what that means. Let me tell you about living for years with your children blaming you for the divorce or blaming you in general because of your inability to go through it and come out the other side intact enough to be a good parent, or to be a good anything, for a while, for that matter."

Next, I would tell them about the financial devastation and then try and describe the destruction of you as a person—a thing one can only recognize in retrospect and then it's too late to salvage the respect of your children.

There are many valid reasons for the failure of my first marriage, reasons that ran much deeper than what was obvious to friends and family. Even our children can see that we had nothing in common. If he were asked why, I'm sure his answers would be different from mine and neither would be completely true or false. If I told you that he was unfaithful, I believe that would be true, and if I told you that was why we divorced that also would be both the truth *and* a lie.

I spent much of that married life believing that I was not really in love with my husband, that I had only married him to get away from "mommy dearest." I didn't know it at the time but that was also both truth and a lie.

Later in life the term "in love" took on a different meaning. It now reminds me of someone who "got religion"; the initial ardor of which soon fades. I have come to understand that genuine love and integrity are more closely aligned—it's more about keeping promises than it is about keeping feelings. Any intimacy that endures is achieved through trust and respect.

My husband often told our friends that I was a great mother, a wonderful cook and the best housekeeper but not a very good wife. He was telling the truth. I was a terrible wife, not because I didn't care but because I simply didn't know how.

I grew up in a house of storm shielded only by an imaginary veil made up of daydreams, pulled over my head like a lead blanket of protection between myself and the fallout of my parent's fighting. My father was often angry and, when he wasn't, my mother was relentless in her efforts to pick a fight. It seemed as if chaos was the only thing she knew.

The only marriages I had seen up close, like those of my parents and grandparents, didn't exactly equip me with the tools necessary for making a good marriage. My grandmother was more like a servant than a wife. My mother kept an argument open constantly. Arguing looked like the better role to me than servitude, so I chose that one, but I didn't scream and yell like my mother. What I did was probably more destructive—I was critical of everything my husband did, from his table manners to the way he talked and much more.

In every other aspect of my married life I turned myself inside out to create an appearance of perfection. My husband had a great job and loved his girls and provided for us very well. Our children were well behaved and good looking. I was always ready to appear in public at a moment's notice. He could bring a guest home at the last minute and never fear being embarrassed. Our home was beautiful and spotlessly clean.

In those days, I can never remember yelling at the children. If the phone rang and the call was for someone else, I walked to wherever that person was and quietly told them they had a phone call. Underneath that outward appearance, however, was an angry and hurt woman. I must have been choking to death on all that perfection. Can you imagine how much energy it took to keep up the facade?

I loved my home and worked to protect the image I had created. I'm not a stupid woman and I'm sure that, on some level, I suspected my husband was, and had always been, unfaithful. Perhaps if I had taken a closer look, I would have seen the truth other people could already see. But I didn't want to see the truth and I was desperate to keep my illusions alive.

Our deepest motives are often opaque to introspection. I have understood that since long before I was mature enough to have acquired the vocabulary with which to express it. I could have believed anything if a lie better armed me in my fight to hold my family together. A motivation that strong can cause one to be blind to almost anything.

When our house of cards ultimately came crashing down I should have been ready, but I wasn't. After he moved out I spent many nights with the covers over my head so my daughters wouldn't hear me crying. I was stunned by the depth of my grief, which was not what would be expected from a wife who didn't love her husband.

A few weeks later he made a trip to Pennsylvania and came back with a complete change of heart. By that time I had been through the worst of the pain and was already emotionally "out the door," just waiting for the paper work from the lawyers to catch up.

In an attempt to force me to take him back, he stopped giving me money. I often found myself, after the girls were asleep, looking through old purses and the pockets of coats and under chair cushions for enough change to pay for their lunches at school the next day. Everyone commented about how much weight I had lost, never realizing it was because I didn't have money for food. Finally, after three weeks of those tactics, my soon-to-be ex-husband learned that my brother was coming for a visit. He didn't want to be embarrassed, so he showed up at the house with bags of groceries.

I don't recall how long it took for the divorce to be finalized. In the interim I found two part time jobs and put the house on the market. I soon had a sales contract but the sale didn't close for five long months. Fortunately, we lived in a small town and I knew the banker who allowed me to wait until the closing to make up the five months of late mortgage payments.

The first time I saw my little girl walk into a movie theatre with her father without me, it hurt so much I couldn't breathe. I was with some girlfriends but there was no distraction great enough to lessen the pain of feeling like an outsider in what had been my family, the center of my world. Whenever I allow a rare reflection on those awful times I still can't get that picture out of my mind. At the time, I used every ounce of strength I could muster to keep from crying in front of my friends.

I don't know why I couldn't admit even to close friends how broken I was. Maybe it was due to pride but I never told anyone how much I missed him. I sold our bedroom furniture and bought a smaller bed and covered it with only feminine things. I told myself I was glad he was gone, but I knew it was a lie. I knew then that I might never be able to sleep with another man—it would be too much to take the risk of going through the agony of getting used to sleeping alone again. It has been more than 30 years since then and I have learned that my first husband was right about some things—one thing in particular: there is no perfect marriage.

We both have new spouses and we're all friends; at least we're friendly. I'm thankful for that. I see many divorced couples hate each other until one dies and sometimes long afterwards. I also recognize and appreciate that his confession of the truth and his asking for forgiveness made a huge difference in how I feel about him now—it took courage and self-sacrifice for him to do that.

Divorce is a demon, an evil force that causes many people to forget the good times altogether. I have many fond memories of the good times but it was years afterwards before I could fully embrace them again. I especially appreciate memories of our travels and wonderful family traditions started then that I still enjoy. During the years we lived in Turkey, our family began a Christmas tradition of eating a Middle Eastern dinner. I still do that with my daughters and grandchildren whenever possible.

This past Christmas Eve, I asked everyone at the dinner table to tell their favorite memory of family traditions. My son-in-law Jim said his was of opening all of the gifts with his family on Christmas Eve. My granddaughter said hers was of Nana and Gramps being in the driveway waiting for them to wake up on Christmas morning, ready to come in and watch as they opened their Santa gifts. (I was so warmed by her story that I could have stayed up all night to be sure Gary and I arrived on time the next morning.)

My daughter said her favorite memory was of Christmas at Great Grandma's house. I didn't have the heart to tell her that her 34-year-old memory was not aligned with reality, that that visit was not nearly as wonderful as she remembered, at least from my perspective.

I knew because we only spent Christmas with Momie Edna once—the year after George moved out, when Sandi was eight years old. At the last minute, he and I had decided to spend Christmas in the "neutral" setting of my grandmother's house in Kentucky. We packed up the girls, their gifts, a tree, and all the necessary ornaments, and called my grandmother to say that we would arrive the next day.

Funny, the things we remember from childhood. My daughter easily forgot what was painful and now only recalls Momie Edna's excitement. We hadn't told Momie the real reason for the break in our family tradition, which had previously involved staying at home and putting toys together after the girls were in bed. But it had been at her house that I had spent all of my Christmases when I was a child and it seemed like the logical choice for what was to be our last family-style Christmas together. More than anything I wanted to make that last Christmas special. My daughter's memory of it is confirmation that I must have succeeded.

When I was married to George he could do everything around the house from small repairs to building a new deck. He took care of my car and arranged for a friend to help me when he was away on business. I didn't even know how to put gasoline in my car. Shortly after he moved out I found myself in the garage filled with self-pity as I tried to chop kindling wood to build a fire in the fireplace. I felt even more helpless trying to get a large Christmas tree into the stand.

In many ways, my life seemed to be easier before the divorce. Friends and family thought I had made a terrible mistake. I sometimes doubted myself, especially during those first lonely nights, sometimes spending hours talking on the phone to some poorly qualified person working a suicide hot line.

I know people who stayed in their marriages after infidelity and later in life come to think it the best decision they ever made. In my case, it was more the catalyst for ending something that was broken before it began.

In many ways I'm a better person now than I was then. Today I could probably chop down that damn tree and drag it home by myself. I take my own car to the repair shop and can fix almost anything round the house that breaks. I can shoot a gun and I'm better at starting a fire than my Eagle Scout husband. I cannot imagine ever again being dependent on someone else for everything necessary to survive. I like the satisfaction of knowing that I have the ability to make a living and take care of myself.

In my first marriage, the feeling of being trapped was making me physically and emotionally sick. The fact that I feel better now than I did more than 30 years ago tells me that I did the right thing.

Am I a stronger and better person because I didn't stay in a bad marriage? I think so.

MY FATHER'S HAND

I place my hands on the tops of my knees to stop them from shaking but quickly remove them because I fear someone might notice and offer to help me Gripping the back of the pew in front of me, I manage to stand but my knees are too weak to carry me.

In my peripheral vision, I see men moving forward to close the casket. Desperate, I am finally able to take that first step and, miraculously, my legs begin to carry me out of the pew and down the aisle. I didn't ask for help because I needed to be alone to say goodbye. There was no one who could comfort me, nor anyone with whom I could share this private moment. I knew everyone in the church was watching me but I was alone and in complete silence.

My father, the only person in the world whom I trusted, had died on New Year's Eve. I have no memory of returning to my seat but I clearly remember being consumed by a single thought. "This is, and will forever remain, the worst thing that will happen to me in my life."

In my earliest memories, it is my father who stands out as having had the greatest influence on my life. Anything good about myself I learned from him. Even now he keeps me on the right path.

To the casual observer, my work as an interior designer may appear to be a career which consists of nothing more than perpetual shopping. What goes on behind the scenes is far less glamorous. Recently, at the end of a long day, I was making my last stop in preparation for a huge installation the next morning. As I was unloading my purchases into the car, I noticed two cakes of coconut soap at the bottom of my cart, which had been forgotten at check out.

I thought, "I have to keep the soap! It's Doctor Williams' favorite and I promised to find it for her. It's late, I'm tired and the store is about to close anyway. I spent so much money on linens, they should give me the soap."

However, before I finished parking the cart in the return stall, I heard my father's voice. "Girl, you know better than that!" I turned around, headed back to the store and paid for the soap.

As far back as I can remember, when my father said goodbye to me, he would lay his hand on top of my head, and say, "Now, you be a good girl." He continued that ritual until shortly before he died, when I was 34 years old. It would be many years later before I fully understood the significance of that simple gesture.

I thought my father was the most handsome, the smartest, the hardest working man I ever knew. One can tell from the epitaph I selected for his grave marker: "A King of a Man in Honesty and Integrity." Though as I write this I am twice the age I was at the time of his death, I still believe it to be true.

When I was of preschool age, he taught me to count, spell, write and do arithmetic and he gave me wise counsel. "Manners aren't just a set of rules to be memorized—they're a matter of consideration for others." "If you care about other people and their comfort and feelings you are automatically polite." "The thing you dread most tells you exactly what you should do next."

One of my fondest memories is of waking up every morning and rushing to the kitchen door where Dad sat his round dinner bucket when he came home from work late at night. He always left a stick of Beechnut gum in it for me. I still remember how the drinking water in the bottom of the bucket smelled of mint.

I never heard him tell a lie or knew him to break a promise. While Mother practically lived in church, my father only attended sporadically, but he was far more faithful about doing what was right. His integrity was innate. Everyone who knew my father trusted and respected him, and so did I.

Even after I was an adult, I still consulted my father about important matters because I knew that I could count on him to tell me the truth, even when it wasn't easy for me to hear. When my husband and I bought our first house, we asked him for his opinion before signing the sales contract. As we showed him through the house and yard I waited with baited breath for his response. Finally, he said, with mock seriousness. "There is only one thing wrong with this house—it isn't on my property." We had his approval!

About a year after we moved into that new home, I became pregnant with our second child. As soon as Dad learned that we were expecting again, he showed up with all the necessary tools to build a fence around our very large back yard. By noon of the first day he had dug thirty post holes before taking a break for lunch. When my husband came home from work that day, the posts were set, ready for the fencing to be installed the next day. That would have been an incredible task for any ordinary man but for my father it was extraordinary—as you recall, he had only one hand.

One day, I was outside playing with my friend Bobby Elswick and he said, "How did your daddy get his arm broke off?" Confused, I went flying home to confirm that Daddy did, indeed, have an arm missing. And I recall once when my brother and I were sitting with Dad at a singing convention at church. Everyone applauded after each soloist or singing group performed. Several times I said, "Clap, Daddy, clap." Haford looked at me as if I were an idiot. And I sure felt like one when I saw the look on my father's face. Because he worked harder than most men with two hands, I sometimes forgot and said foolish things. It didn't occur to me that he was handicapped in any way. To this day I cringe when I remember doing that.

Soon after Dad died, when my daughters were eight and fifteen, my first husband and I divorced. I was frantic about the settlement, and I had reason to worry, but in an effort to win my trust, George shared a story with me.

"Do you remember that Christmas Day, a few days before your dad died, when we were leaving the hospital and he asked me to come back into the room?"

I nodded that I did.

"When I stepped back to his bedside, he said, 'I want you to promise me that you will take care of Nadine no matter what happens.'

"'Of course, I will, Curtis,' I said, 'I always have.'

"Then your dad said, 'I'm not sure you understand what I'm asking. I'm saying I want your *word* that you will take care of her no matter what happens.'"

"So, you see, even if I didn't want to treat you fairly, I know that, somehow, Curtis would haunt me."

After the divorce, I found single parenting and a new career overwhelming. I had finished design training and had a job in a department store design studio and was also trying to sell real estate. But in the late 1970s, when mortgage interest rates climbed into the double digits, home and property sales were almost non-existent. Eventually, I procured a contract as a manufacturer's representative to sell noise abatement and ventilation materials for use in deep mines and at coal preparation plants. I used my maiden name when I had my business cards printed.

Every Monday morning, I put on a hard hat, jeans and boots and traveled all over West Virginia and parts of Pennsylvania making sales calls. I'll never forget the day one of those old prep-plant superintendents looked at my card and then back up at me.

"You any kin to Curtis Justice?" he asked.

"Yes sir," I said, "That's my daddy."

Until that moment, I had been just another salesperson. I watched the expression on his weathered face change, and knew just what he was thinking. "Here's Curtis' girl trying to make a living for her children and working hard just like her dad. Let's help her out."

Thanks to the man my father was, I sold Brattice cloth and noise abatement materials until I was able to sell the house and get out of West Virginia. It was a good thing, too. After our divorce, my ex-husband started a new business that didn't work out. In spite of his good intentions and the promise he'd made to my father, he was often not able to pay child support.

Many years after Dad died, and I had moved to Atlanta, I still missed him. Without the benefit of his wise counsel, I also made some very poor choices. One was marrying a good looking, successful man who proved to be unlike my father, in every possible way.

One Sunday my new husband and I took his twelve-year-old daughter to a matinee at the Fox Theatre. During intermission, I went downstairs to the ladies room and they went outside to wait where he could smoke a cigarette. A discussion ensued between them about plans for the upcoming summer's vacation. Just as I came outside to rejoin them, I overheard her say, "Do we have to take her with us?"

I had tried my best to win over this child and was deeply hurt by her rejection. I managed to keep from crying until we were again seated and the lights were dimmed. I looked up at the Theatre's man-made sky of magical twinkling stars and animated clouds, while still fighting back tears. At that very moment, I felt a hand on the top of my head as real as if my father had been physically present.

I immediately experienced such a feeling of peace and calm that I knew nothing could hurt me. And I understood that my father was still watching over me.

The time of my life
In relation to the world
Is insignificant

The time spent with you
In relation to my life
Was brief—
      but not insignificant

—Javan—

PAULEY

The first time I ever saw him he was the speaker at our monthly sorority meeting. I can't remember the topic but after the meeting, several (actually, most...) of the women swarmed around him like bees to honeysuckle vine—each asking inane questions, clearly designed to try and get his attention.

I found it amusing but, except for taking discreet notice of the fact that he might have been the best looking man I had ever seen, I otherwise paid little attention to him. I gathered my belongings, and then left, basically forgetting the evening—except for his voice, which I was destined to remember for the rest of my life.

Soon afterwards, my friend Jessica told me he had asked her for my phone number. I suspected that his inquiry had little to do with any real attraction to me, that his interest had been piqued because I was the only female in the room who didn't make a fuss over him. It was obvious that he was accustomed to having lots of attention from women. In any case, I wouldn't allow Jess to give him my phone number.

In spite of that, a few years later he did call me. Even after all that time I recognized the voice immediately. We talked on the phone that Sunday afternoon for at least three hours. I think I could have talked for three days non-stop and would have felt like it was only the beginning of what I wanted to tell him. I had never before in my life felt so immediately safe and comfortable with another human being. From that day forward it was hard to think about anything else.

The first trip we took together was to Cumberland Park in Kentucky. I had put a lot of thought into planning the trip and wanted everything to be perfect. Jess was glad to keep the kids so I wasn't worried about them but still I was a nervous wreck. You see, I hadn't been divorced very long from a marriage that had lasted almost seventeen years and I had never been to bed with any man other than my husband. To say that I was anxious about spending three days alone in a secluded cabin with this gorgeous man would be a huge understatement.

In spite of those best laid plans nearly everything that could go wrong did. I had assumed that there would be a grocery store, wine shop, and our pick of restaurants nearby. I was wrong on all counts. Those were the days before MapQuest so by the time we finally found the check-in office, picked up our key and located our cabin, the few local retail establishments were closing. To make matters worse, as it turned out, this place was located in a dry county. That nice bottle of wine to go with the gourmet dinner I had planned to cook was also out of the question. It no longer mattered anyway since the closest stores were now closed and it was too late to backtrack to a larger town.

After we unpacked the car and Pauley had built a fire in the wood burning fireplace I went into the bathroom to freshen up and discovered, to my dismay, that I had started my period a week early. I was mortified, but will never forget his response to the whole episode. He just burst out laughing that incredible laugh of his (I can still hear it every time I think of him). "Well," he said, "Here we are with nothing to eat, nothing to drink and," looking pointedly in my direction, "Nothing to do."

I don't recall what we did about dinner that first night but do remember that we dragged a mattress down from one of the upstairs bedrooms and placed it on the floor in front of the huge stone fireplace with the roaring fire, where we slept for the remainder of our stay.

I hardly slept at all that first night but we got up the next morning to discover a beautiful and unexpected snowfall. A raccoon looked in at us through the glass door leading to the deck, and we rushed to the windows just in time to spot deer, a fox and some other wild life. The deer looked back at us as if to say, "This is our home. You're just visiting, and don't you forget it."

We quickly dressed in our warmest clothes and took a walk by the most beautiful lake and pristine woods I have ever seen. Then we went out to shop for groceries, found a wine shop in a nearby town, and stopped for brunch at a great little hole-in-the-wall. I cooked for him over the next two days, to show off my culinary skills, and the effort was appropriately rewarded. He was duly impressed.

The trip, that got off to a rough start, smoothed out nicely and turned into a great experience after all. However, we were only able to stay for two of the three days I had reserved because, when I called to check on my children, both of them were home from school with the flu.

We continued to date for the next four years but had no definitive plans for marriage—at least I didn't. Married too young the first time, I felt as if I had just escaped from prison and didn't want to return. At least that's what I told people, and myself, when I had to explain my hesitation. I suspect the truth of the matter was that I was just plain scared to death.

I think I believed that he would leave me, and that I would shrivel up and die or break into a million little pieces. I don't know exactly what I feared. I only know that after we finally got married I did about everything possible to sabotage our marriage.

I had not yet realized that in the arena of love relationships I had been mortally wounded, which rendered me incapable of sustaining a marriage. When he left—or more accurately, when I had succeeded in chasing him away, I did all the usual stupid things people do to anesthetize themselves. It was several years before I finally stopped running and grieved the great loss of what I had killed.

As I've grown older and wiser, I've come to understand that most of what happens to us in life is a direct result of our own choices, reactions and attitudes which are directed by past experiences. Blaming others is the demon that deceives and it's only when we remain alert to this fact that we can make a conscious effort to avoid the pitfalls. That knowledge brings with it some peace and freedom, useful in the present, and provides a measure of security for the future. But it can also intensify the pain of regret.

All the years for me since haven't been empty for many reasons, including occasional contact from him. After I left West Virginia he came to Tennessee to see me on his Harley because he "just happened" to be taking a ride through the Smokey Mountains. Several years after that, he showed up in Atlanta on a beautiful black Goldwing because he "just happened" to be in my area en route to the North Georgia mountains.

During one of our rare lengthy phone conversations a few years ago, he allowed me the opportunity to apologize. He offered his forgiveness, assuring me that he knew that my failing was not because I didn't love him. I will always be grateful to him for that.

In a letter he wrote after he left, he said that we were once the best of everything a couple could hope to be. I've also been told that he still freely tells people that I was the love of his life. I know that is true. I also know that's all in the past and we can't have it back. But I sometimes wish I could discreetly drive by the mountaintop horse farm where he now lives and have a close-up look at the log house he chinked with his own hands. I picture him standing there smiling, as if he knew I might one day show up.

One of my Christmas gifts every year has been the anticipation of a phone call I can always count on getting from him. I haven't heard from him in a long time but I sometimes wonder if when he looks out on fallen snow he thinks of me.

In areas of life
Where reason controls
We usually learn from our mistakes
Unfortunately
This is not always true
In areas where emotion controls

— Javan —

MEN AND MARRIAGE

I rarely speak of my second marriage. Sometimes a thing is too delicate to examine in the light of day and too important to hold up for possible criticism by people who could not possibly understand. So I'll tell you about my other relationships with men; the ones I married and the ones I had the good sense not to marry.

As you might imagine, after that second failed marriage, I was heartbroken. But instead of grieving in an honest and healing manner, I tried to escape my private hell by putting up a front. I soon found myself behaving like my mother—something I had, of course, vowed never to do. In a short time, I learned that unless you're scarred and scared enough, you can't know what you might do to kill pain.

After a few years of looking for love in all the wrong places, and making equally wrong choices, I sold my house in West Virginia and moved to Atlanta. I was excited about making a fresh start and promised myself that I would be more discriminating with respect to men. I would be careful about forming friendships too quickly. I would date only men who possessed the qualities I most admired. I wanted a man who was refined, successful, intelligent, educated, socially sophisticated and trustworthy. It was a short list—how hard could it be? I would soon find out.

First, I met a man who "put on his best face" for two rather pleasant dates. On our third date, however, I looked across the table to find him scratching his head, chewing with his mouth wide open, talking all the while. Suddenly, in place of this man's face, I saw the image of Jack, our old family dog.

We never allowed our dogs to come inside the house when I was growing up—it was considered "uncivilized." It was a sign, I thought, so in an effort to make it through the remainder of the evening without being rude—or becoming ill—I tried to concentrate on positive things.

At least, unlike ol' Jack, it's his head that he's scratching, I told myself. I have motivation to skip dessert—I'm slightly cross-eyed, so he won't notice that every time he takes a bite of food large enough to change the shape of his face, I'm looking over his shoulder to avoid looking at him. My house is only fifteen minutes away. I won't be expected to invite him in because tomorrow is a work day.

So much for refined. Having escaped from that potential disaster, I looked for someone better educated and found a man who had graduated *magna cum laude* from Wharton. Admittedly, we had deep, meaningful and intellectual conversations, but he couldn't figure out how to support himself financially, not to mention his ex-wife and three children.

So I set my sights for "trustworthy," And met a retired minister. After we dated for several months, he declared that he was in love with me and I was thrilled.

Soon afterwards, he had to go out of town on business—with a female co-worker whom he said he detested. On the afternoon of his departure, he left me a voice mail message to say that his flight had been delayed.

When I came home from work that evening I returned his call. When he answered his phone, I heard him whisper, "I'll be right back." He told me that he was still at the Atlanta airport, known as the busiest airport in the world, and yet the entire time we talked, I did not hear a single sound in the background. No flight announcements, no anything. So much for trustworthy.

As I said, I had hoped to have the good fortune of finding a man who was successful and blessed with all the other desirable attributes as well. I thought that good fortune had come when I met a very bright and educated man, who owned a thriving business, had impeccable manners, a designer wardrobe and was a wonderful dancer. He was a brilliant conversationalist and romantic to a fault—even wrote beautiful poetry. We went to formal dances at the Ritz Carlton and vacationed in exotic places. (Five thousand dollar shopping trips at Neiman's didn't hurt his image either.)

I loved the excitement and glamour but sensed something wrong and decided to stop seeing him. When he asked why, I replied, "I'm not sure, but I have an uneasy feeling that I shouldn't trust you."

"Just give me a chance and I will prove to you that I'm trustworthy," he promised.

And he set out to do just that. Every Monday morning, he had Amelia roses delivered to my office—you know, the big, beautiful, white ones with just a hint of pink? Perfection! As brilliant as he was, he did not seem to notice that all of his extravagant gifts and wining and dining only served to convey that he was rich.

I, on the other hand, was a struggling single parent. I can't distinguish when or where that inner warning caved in to "here is a man who is capable and willing to take care of me and my daughter," but from a position of scared, lonely and insecure, he started looking pretty good. And, of course, I married him.

I was able to quit my downtown job and concentrate on redecorating the home we bought on the golf course in the country club community where he was a member. Then, just when I was getting used to the new life style, truth reared its ugly head. To my horror, my publicly stylish husband, a recovering alcoholic with fourteen years of sobriety, was secretly using illegal drugs.

I soon moved out and filed for divorce, vowing to never marry again. For a few years after that, I concentrated on work and building an interior design business. But living alone was neither as much fun nor as freeing as I had expected it to be. Though stuck at an age where celibacy could still make one crazy, it was at a time in the world—during the mid eighties—when sex could kill you. Literally.

My friends and co-workers, either envious or judgmental, commented on how many different suitors I had. Whether they were expressing envy or judgment, they did not understand a third date seemed to come with an unspoken rule—known only to men—of an invitation to bed. For that reason, I rarely got beyond a third date.

Every time, after a brief swearing-off-men-altogether period I would, invariably, accept an invitation to a concert, movie, or dinner with some nice gentleman, usually someone I met at church. I quickly learned that meeting them at church was no guarantee at all—of anything.

Eventually, after several short-lived and shallow relationships, I did get married again, this time to a man who did not attend my church. The first Monday morning after our brief honeymoon, I was eager to get back into my work routine. I made coffee and scones, had breakfast, took my shower and was ready to start work. He slowly ate breakfast and watched the news.

I kept glancing in his direction. With rising panic, I saw him pour a third cup of coffee. "When is he going to leave for home so I can get to work?" I thought.

That's when reality hit me like a ton of bricks. "Oh no! I married him! He's never going home!"

When he finally stepped into the shower, I headed upstairs to my office to tackle the stack of work that had piled up in the past several weeks. By the time I had finished clearing off my desk I had tripped over his exercise bench three times. "Where am I supposed to put this man and his stuff?"

As days went on, he started trying to change me and I began my own "remodel job" on him. Neither of us were having any real success, and I suspected he wasn't any happier than I was.

Whereas he had been married for thirty-four years to a domesticated house wife, I had spent several years as a single parent, had finally become an independent woman, and was running a busy and successful business.

His efforts to change me were no less subtle than mine—just different. It was obvious that I was not the wife he had expected, and in an effort to whip me into shape, he began telling me stories about what his ex-wife had done for him.

While we were dating he hadn't said a kind word about the woman, but now she became the quintessential wife, practically a saint. She always had something sweet baked for him. She was very thin. (He had once described her as being so skinny he didn't find her appealing.) She was always perfectly groomed. She liked doing the same things he did, including watching football. (I hate football.) Their house was immaculate. She was frugal and never hired a cleaning service (like I do).

When he had finished his last glowing report, hoping that I would see the error of my ways, I looked him square in the eyes and said, "You're really going to miss that woman. In fact, though I've never met her, I miss her myself. Do you think you could get her to come here and do all of that stuff for us?"

He was not amused.

Before we married, I had bought a house—a patio home in a lake community—with good bones and thirty foot high ceilings. I had transformed it from a space that was almost uninhabitable into a lovely, glamorous home. I began to feel confined and made a hasty decision to sell it, a decision I would later regret when I realized my feeling trapped had nothing to do with that house, or any for that matter.

Though I wasn't sure I wanted to stay married to him, every time I introduced him to friends or family members, they almost always said, "What a nice guy. You really found a good one this time." With each new compliment he received, I panicked even more.

Before we married, he had told me that it just "killed" him if people didn't like him, and because of it, he would do most anything he thought would make them like him. I should have listened. As soon as we were married, he no longer felt the need to win me over—that job was finished. I thought he was a nice guy too but he began to ignore me and was sometimes even rude to me when I tried to participate in his focused and self-promotional conversations with other people.

I became resentful, and the more my friends and family patted him on the back the further I retreated. I became lonelier and more isolated than I had ever been during my days as a single woman. I could not confide in anyone because they all liked him. I was sure they wouldn't believe he was not the same person at home as the one they saw. After all, he was the "nice guy" with only *one* failed marriage behind him.

Even so, I was determined to make this marriage work. I didn't think I could survive another divorce. I have always been on good terms with my two living ex-husbands, but I suspected another divorce would be a disaster. I had accepted that I could not change him and determined instead to seek counseling for myself. Something had to change—my doctor had warned that I could not remain so intensely unhappy without getting sick.

Fortunately, I found a wonderful, caring and experienced therapist whom I saw on a weekly basis for more than two years. Life, of course, wasn't instantly perfect and I was still often lonely and sad, but I had managed to hold my marriage together.

I began to write these memoirs, and with each story, it was as if I was regurgitating things onto the page. Sometimes with tearful resistance, I spent countless hours at our mountain cottage, pouring out onto paper scenes from my childhood and teenage years. It has been one of the most purifying and therapeutic exercises of my life.

As I learned to be less critical of myself, I realized that I was also becoming more accepting of the imperfections of others, especially those I perceived in my husband. I began to focus more on his positive qualities as well.

At some point in the process of writing memoir I looked up, took a good look around me, and was astounded by how much my husband had changed in just a few short years!

JUDY AND KENNETH

*I*t was a little after five o'clock on a Saturday afternoon and I had just walked in the door, home from work. It was a rather ordinary day...until five minutes later, when my daughter Sherrie's husband Michael called from Kentucky.

"Nadine, this is Michael. Sherrie and Marshall are fine but I have some bad news."

"Oh, no," I think, "maybe he's calling to say George has had a heart attack. This family isn't ready for that." Though George was my ex-husband, he was still my children's father and they were close to him.

Then Michael continued. "Kenny has had a car wreck."

"How bad is it," I say, and "where is he?"

"As bad as it can be. He's gone."

"What do you mean, gone?"

"He was killed," he said, "and Sandi doesn't know yet, so you will have to tell her."

"Oh, dear God," I think, "how can I tell my child that her brother is dead?"

My girls had always wanted a little brother so when George and Judy had gotten together, the fact that she had a five-year-old son was just fine with them. Judy was a pretty cool lady in her own right and the girls liked her immediately, too, partly because, unlike their father's previous girlfriends, she didn't do phony things to try and win them over. Judy was comfortable enough in her own skin to allow things to develop naturally and in an appropriate time frame.

However, the real attraction for my daughters was her little boy Kenny—Sandi and Sherrie adored him. If either of them went on a trip and only had money to buy one thing, it would invariably be spent on a gift for him. I never heard either of them, from the day they met him, refer to Kenny as anything except "my brother."

I kept asking Michael how Sherrie was—I was really worried about her. I asked him if she could talk, and he put her on the phone. After I was satisfied she was all right, I picked up the phone to call Judy's mother Eunice.

She sounded surprisingly strong—surprising until later. After I had time to reflect, I realized that as much as Eunice loved her grandson, it was for her own child that she reached to find strength deep within herself. Judy was going to need her now more than ever in her life.

I then called *my* mother, and, after she regained her composure, we cried and prayed together for the entire family and for the strength I would need to complete the bitter task before me. Immediately after I hung up from talking to Mother, the phone rang. It was Sandi.

She began telling me about some new clothes she had bought. I interrupted her to say that I was going to be coming out her way in a few minutes and would love to stop in and see her new things. Oblivious, she protested that her apartment was a mess and that it might be better if she came to see me, instead. I insisted that since I would be driving right by, it only made sense that I come to see her.

She could tell by the tone in my voice that something was wrong, so it was with a great deal of effort that I finally convinced her that I was fine and would see her in about twenty minutes. I told her that I didn't even need to come in.

That drive seemed like the longest twenty minutes of my life. As I entered Sandi's apartment complex, she was just parking her car and

I pulled in beside her. Without pausing for breath, she began again, telling me about her newly acquired purchases.

After a minute or two, I finally stopped her. "Sandi, something has happened." Like me, her first thought was that it was her father. "No," I said. "It's Kenny. He had a car accident and the news is very bad."

She was frozen. "Is he alive?"

"No, Honey, he's not."

The look on her face and the image of her sinking to the pavement, as she absorbed that news, will be indelibly imprinted in my mind forever.

When Judy and Kenny came into their lives, I was happy that my children finally had a brother but I was especially grateful for George's good judgment in his choice of a new mate. If I had been given the privilege of selecting someone for the position of stepmother for my children, I could not have done a better job.

Judy is the most non-judgmental and balanced person I have ever met, and a much better fit for George than I ever was. I often joke that if she hadn't married my husband, she would have been my best friend. That remark draws laughter at family gatherings, but we all know it's probably true.

A few years ago, my best friend's mother died and I went back to West Virginia for the funeral. Sandi decided that she and the kids would go along and visit with her father while I paid my respects to Lena's family and spent time with other friends.

At the beginning of our trip, when I stopped at their house to pick them up, my grandchildren, Chase and Chloe came running, dragging their little suitcases behind them, excited about going on a trip to visit their *other* grandparents.

"Nana," they asked, "do you know our Papaw? If you don't, we'll introduce you when we get there." We all laughed, never bothering to try and explain just how well I *did* know their grandfather.

To make matters even more interesting, our somewhat unusual

family unit now includes Gary, my current husband, who has come to enjoy the benefits of our relationship as well. George makes great peanut butter fudge, which is Gary's favorite. So when they come to Atlanta to visit the kids, *one* of my husbands brings the *other* a big plate of homemade fudge.

Several months after Kenny died, when our second grandson Zachary was born, I couldn't help being acutely aware of how difficult it must have been for Judy. In spite of my joy, I kept wondering what she was thinking and feeling. I found myself occasionally glancing in her direction and, seeing the look of pain on her face, would say a silent prayer for her.

It may seem odd to people outside our family circle to see us together when there is a family event to be celebrated or mourned. But what other people think isn't what is important to me. I'm grateful that whether we've gathered for a wedding, a funeral or a baptism, or are pacing in a hospital waiting room, my children need never be stressed over where to seat their parents in order to keep the peace.

The night Chase and Chloe were born, my son-in-law Jim dashed outside the O.R. to inform their *six* waiting grandparents that they had arrived and that everything was fine. I kept asking how my daughter was, but in all of the excitement I thought no one heard me. I broke away from the group and walked down an empty hallway to have good cry of relief. I felt a hand on my back, and turned around to find Judy there, ready with a hug and a kind comment.

Then, when my mother died, I again felt a hand on my shoulder and looked up to see her. She hugged me and said, "I can't imagine both of my parents gone."

Rarely a day goes by when Judy is not in my thoughts. I thank God for the role she has played in my children's lives and the graciousness with which she became a member not only of their family, but mine. And I pray that our grandchildren help to lessen the pain of her great loss.

ON FRIENDSHIP
Kahlil Gibran

Your friend is your needs answered.
He is your field which you sow with love and reap with thanksgiving.
And he is your board and your fireside.
For you come to him with your hunger, and you seek him for peace.

When your friend speaks his mind you fear not the "nay" in your own
mind, nor do you withhold the "ay."
And when he is silent your heart ceases not to listen to his heart;
For without words, in friendship, all thoughts, all desires, all expectations
are born and shared, with joy that is unacclaimed.

When you part from your friend, you grieve not;
For that which you love most in him may be clearer in his absence, as the
mountain to the climber is clearer from the plain.

And let there be no purpose in friendship save the deepening of the spirit.
For love that seeks aught but the disclosure of its own mystery is not love
but a net cast forth: and only the unprofitable is caught.

And let your best be for your friend.
If he must know the ebb of your tide, let him know its flood also.

For what is your friend that you should seek him with hours to kill?
Seek him always with hours to live.
For it is his to fill your need, but not your emptiness.

And in the sweetness of friendship let there be laughter, and sharing of
pleasures. For in the dew of little things the heart finds its morning and is
refreshed.

MARY ANN

*W*hen I moved to Atlanta more than 25 years ago, I obviously could not bring my clients with me so I had to start my business again from scratch. I was a single parent with one child still at home and in high school and was in no position to wait around. Fortunately, I was able to secure a job with an employment agency until I could rebuild my client list.

On my first day of work, I met Mary Ann. She was kind and helpful and I really needed a friend at the time. We became very close, and remained so, long after we found new jobs that took us in opposite directions, both geographically and in category.

Mary Ann was tall, slim and beautiful, and more fun than any woman I had ever met. The first day we met she was wearing black slacks, high heels and a pink and black polka dot blouse cut just low enough.

She left work early that day to pick up her husband at the airport. He had been away working in Saudi Arabia and she hadn't seen him in almost six months. Was he in for a surprise! (She had recently had a breast augmentation without telling him.)

On Monday morning when she came back to work I asked about Denny's reaction.

"He said, 'Whatever you paid was worth every penny," she said. I can still hear the way she laughed when she told that story around the office that day. We both lived in Lilburn (GA) at that time and visited often, especially on weekends. Later, when I remarried and moved to Roswell, we were both very busy with our respective careers and it wasn't as easy to get together. We always managed to, however, even though it would sometimes be March before we celebrated Christmas and exchanged our gifts.

She was an amazing friend who was always by my side through good times and bad. I never felt alone knowing I could always count on Mary Ann and her faithful friendship. When I left "what's-his-name" and moved out of a beautiful home to a small, rented townhouse, it was she who came to my rescue. I had barely arrived home from work and was feeling overwhelmed by all the boxes stacked around me, when I looked out the kitchen window to see her walking across my lawn, waving a bottle of wine, and laughing that beautiful laugh. She had come to help me unpack.

On another occasion, after my daughter Sandi graduated from college and had moved back to Atlanta, she was unhappy with her first job and had asked me to critique her resume before she began actively looking for something else. We met at a restaurant near Mary Ann's house and asked her to join us. Over dinner I read aloud and critiqued Sandi's resume, then turned to Mary Ann and said, "I would hire her. Wouldn't you?" Early the next morning, before going in to work, Mary Ann called to ask if I thought Sandi would be interested in working for her. Sandi was, Mary Ann did hire her and they too became fast friends.

Occasionally, Mary Ann and I went shopping together and once, on a lark, we bought matching dresses with the express promise to each other never to wear them to the same place at the same time. The dresses were black knit with epaulets on the shoulders. One evening we met after work for dinner and, as fate would have it, we were both wearing those darned dresses. Our server at the Blue Ribbon Grill asked what airline we worked for. We just stared at her for a long moment then burst out laughing. She thought we were flight attendants.

The last time I met Mary Ann for lunch I remember watching her, as she walked toward me from across the parking lot, and thinking how beautiful she looked and how much I loved her. Little did I know that a few short weeks later she would be diagnosed with cancer and would die only five months later.

Every year on March 9th, Mary Ann's birthday, I have a dinner party to honor my friend. Because her favorite color was purple I always have purple party decorations and matching flowers on the table. Sandi, Denny, their son and granddaughter and a few of Mary Ann's closest friends—about a dozen in all—show up to celebrate Mary Ann's life. An amazing thing happened at the first annual dinner party—almost everyone, without being prompted, was dressed in purple!

For the last "Purple Party" I had saved a three- litre bottle of wine I had bought at a Charity auction. Sandi came to help me with last minute preparations and just as I was about to open the wine to allow it to breathe, it occurred to me that I should check with a local wine shop as to the actual value before opening it. I had paid $200 and was okay with that for such a special occasion. The wine shop owner said he didn't have that particular varietal but promised to check around and get back to me. When it was nearing the time for guests to arrive I went ahead and opened the wine.

Of course, I didn't answer the phone during dinner. The meal was a hit and the wine thoroughly enjoyed to the last drop. After everyone left and Sandi and I were cleaning up, I decided to check phone messages. The man from the wine shop had left a message to say, "Ms. Justice, do not open that wine, it's a collector's item!" I then went online and found the exact same wine on an auction site stating the most recent bid at $1,099."

Sandi and I stared at each other in disbelief. Then she said, "Mom, don't you know Mary Ann is up there laughing like crazy right now?"

I kept the bottle as a souvenir and every time I look at it I'm reminded of my friend and the fun times we had.

Mary Ann on our trip to
Jamaica together

TWEETIE

It was on moving day that I first met her. We were having a beautiful blue-skied October day, like many in Atlanta. My daughter had come to help and, at some point between trips to carry in another load of boxes, Sandi introduced me to my new neighbors. Standing at my door, and already engaged in lively conversation, was an adorable elderly couple. Bob was tall and elegant; Tweetie was petite and polite. She offered a heartfelt welcome and a fresh baked loaf of banana bread.

I had never met anyone named Tweetie but resisted the temptation to ask if that was her real name. I later learned that indeed it was and that her maiden name was Davis. She, good naturedly, said I could just call her "Tweetie D." (Of course, I didn't.) Tweetie and Bob gave me their phone number and invited me to call on them if I needed anything before making a quick exit so that we could get back to work.

Neither Tweetie nor I knew it then, but it was no accident that I was led to buy the house next door to her. We were going to need each other—my mother had died earlier in the year and Bob would pass away the following January.

My birthday is August 31, the same day as Bob's, and Tweetie's was August 13. We soon learned that we had many things in common, such as a love for watermelon, tomato sandwiches, and fresh coconut cake. We also shared political views and even when I didn't agree,

I pretended to so as not to miss out on some lively discussion of a subject. I loved her "enthusiastic" opinions.

By springtime of the following year, I had finished most of an extensive interior renovation and had begun to tackle the exterior and the yard. One Sunday afternoon, upon discovering I had misplaced my pruning shears, I went next door to borrow a pair. When Tweetie finally came to the door (I knew that she didn't hear well so I always rang the bell and knocked loudly several times), it was obvious that she had been crying. When she went out to the garage to fetch the shears, I noticed a photo album open on the table. I didn't know exactly what to say without treading on what appeared to be a private moment. I thanked her and said that I only needed a few minutes to complete my project. That wasn't completely true—what I really needed was time to try and think of a way to comfort her without being intrusive.

I went home and waited for what seemed like a legitimate length of time and repeated the exercise of getting Tweetie to the door, stepping back after knocking and ringing so that she could see me through the peep hole. As I handed back the borrowed tool, I told her that I was in the mood to see a movie and go out to dinner and I asked her to join me. Upon checking show times in the newspaper, I discovered that every movie showing was either of the "Star Wars" type, made for children, or R-rated. She said she had never seen an R rated movie and wasn't about to start. I suggested instead that we go out to dinner and she invited me to watch a Hallmark or Masterpiece Theatre movie Bob had recorded.

When we discovered that our favorite restaurant at the Holiday Inn around the corner was closed on Sunday, we decided we preferred our own cooking anyway and went back to her house. I don't remember what we had for dinner but do recall that our joint efforts produced an enjoyable meal, made more so by a shared bottle of wine. That was the first of several times I watched "The Ginger

Tree" with her. To this day it is still one of the all time best movies I have ever seen.

I was with Tweetie, too, the night of Princess Diana's fatal accident. I had taken my husband-to-be over for her approval, though, of course, he didn't know it. She made dinner for us and afterwards we watched "The Ginger Tree" again. As soon as the movie finished and we returned to regular programming, the sad news of Princess Diana's accident was filling the airwaves. I learned in church the next morning that she had died.

The year after Gary and I married, we bought another house in the same neighborhood, which was situated on a lot large enough for us to build on a design studio for me. Tweetie took the news as if I were moving to another planet but never wavered in her friendship. In fact, she came over to help me pack my crystal and china. From ten o'clock in the morning until six o'clock that evening we wrapped and packed, taking only a short break for lunch. When we finally finished, Tweetie dusted her dainty hands together and said, "Now what can we do?"

"I don't know about you but I want to quit," I said, "because I'm exhausted." I ordered a pizza and we had dinner together one last time in the dining room by the wood burning fireplace.

After moving a mile away I couldn't as easily walk next door to see Tweetie but we still managed to have many good times together. The year she turned ninety and I sixty, we decided to celebrate our respective August birthdays together by taking a trip. She didn't want to go anywhere she and Bob had traveled and told me that she had always dreamed of taking a trip on the famed Orient Express.

The Orient Express wasn't in my budget, but we decided on Canada, a place neither of us had been before, and we booked a tour through the Canadian Rocky Mountains on the "Rocky Mountain Rail."

When the date arrived for our trip we flew from Atlanta to Seattle and took a shuttle bus on to Vancouver where we spent two days covering the highlights of that city. We both loved Vancouver. On the third day we boarded our train, for the first of a two day spectacular experience through the Canadian Rockies. We had upgraded to the "gold leaf" status which included prime seats on the upper level of a travel car featuring a glass domed ceiling.

We reclined in the luxuriously comfortable seats to enjoy the amazing view as we sipped champagne and wine served by attentive young people who paid special attention to Tweetie. Our every meal, in the dining car on the lower level, was of gourmet quality. It clearly required a pre-engineered plan of enormous precision by the staff to pull off scheduling and serving our train load of tourists. As one filled dining car of people exited to make way for the next car of diners most travelers made a quick stop at the unisex restroom located just outside the dining area and immediately in front of the stairway leading up to our seats. As our group exited the dining car a line formed in front of the restroom.

Tweetie went in before me. We all waited, patiently at first, for what seemed like more than enough time for Tweetie to finish. Gradually the other passengers behind me in line began to shift from one foot to the other and looked in my direction. Eventually, someone said, "Maybe you should check on your friend." I wasn't worried because I knew what was happening—she was brushing and flossing her teeth.

Before I could think of an answer Tweetie appeared all happy and smiling, so I said nothing then, but after she and I returned upstairs and were again settled in our seats, I introduced the idea that perhaps it would be best to skip brushing our teeth so that the line to the restroom could move a little faster. She looked at me with an expression of surprise and said, "Oh, but if I don't brush and floss after every meal I'm not taking care of my teeth." She was ninety years old and still had her own teeth!

At the end of our second day on the train, we arrived in Banff, with plans in place for day trips to see lakes and waterfalls as well as the ice fields. In keeping with the reputation of the Canadian people, our bus driver gave a wary, unfriendly look in Tweetie's direction as we boarded. Our first stop for viewing a spectacular waterfall required a hike of 1½ miles along a narrow and precarious trail on the edge of a cliff. At the end of the trail, we had to duck under a rock opening just large enough for passage out onto a small observation landing. We both stood in awe for a long while, drinking in the wonderful view, before exiting the rock opening and making our way back along the winding trail to re-board the tour bus. At about the half-way point we met the bus driver/tour guide gingerly assisting a large lady who looked to be less than half my little friend's age.

When everyone returned to the bus, the driver turned around, looked at Tweetie and said, "Well, I guess I don't have to worry about you, do I?"

It was hard for me not to laugh out loud.

Two days later we took a shuttle bus to Calgary where we were to board our flight back to Atlanta. Shortly before we arrived at the airport a fierce dust storm blew up from out of nowhere. The driver announced that he would drop off people traveling with small children at their respective airline check-in points, but that all other passengers would have to walk from a central stop.

I cringed at the thought of having sand in my hair and was determined to save the two of us from dragging our bags through a sand storm but I had a problem–Tweetie wouldn't even take advantage of the short line at the voting polls because the rules required her to admit that she was over 75. With some quick thinking I rushed forward, knowing I didn't have time to try and convince her to act as fragile as she looked. I approached the driver and pled my case, namely that my 90-year old mother was not capable of walking any distance. He looked at her and gave me a disgruntled look, but acquiesced. (Luckily, Tweetie didn't hear well and politely fell in step behind me as we made our exit directly in front of the Delta check-in desk.)

Sadly, Tweetie passed away in November 2010, but I see her image in fond memory every day. She was less than five feet tall and didn't weigh a hundred pounds. She was always modestly but tastefully dressed and perfectly groomed. She possessed an abundance of grace, intellect and refinement—qualities that have become all too rare in today's world.

The only health issues she had were caused, not cured, by modern medicine. She lost much of her hearing many years before we met, due to an allergic reaction to an antibiotic. After we became friends, she had cataract surgery and was able to see better than I can. A doctor used acid to remove a mole under her eye and, neglecting to use protective covering, dropped some of the solution into her eye. After months of excruciating pain and a case of shingles, she lost the vision in her right eye.

Until the day she died, Tweetie exercised for 30 minutes every morning before she got out of bed. She said she learned that from her mother and had kept up the regimen all her life.

When her daughters cleaned out her house they found a letter to her late husband among her possessions, entitled "Who Will Hold My Hand?" The few times I saw them together, and in every picture, they were always holding hands. They read it at her graveside memorial, where her ashes were interred beside Bob.

Tweetie and I loved watermelon, so every time I bought one I sliced it down the middle, kept half and took the other half to her. We also shared a love for fresh home grown tomatoes. Whenever I found them at local farmer's markets she and I made white bread, mayonnaise and tomato sandwiches.

I don't know if she believed in an after-life—I never heard her talk about religion. But I *do* think there is a heaven and that she is there now, celebrating and holding hands with Bob again. I hope they're serving tomato sandwiches on white bread, slathered with mayonnaise, and huge, juicy slices of cold watermelon.

And that she's saving some for me.

Tweetie & Bob Schwefel

SUMMER SOLSTICE

*E*very year a group of my mountain girlfriends and I gather to celebrate the day of summer solstice. We dress up in pretty dresses and colorful hats and meet for dinner at a local restaurant. Everyone arrives with a story or poem to read, and a bottle of wine to share. The writings we bring are either our own or ones written by women whom we admire. The occasion is an opportunity for us to catch up on what is happening in each other's lives and to celebrate the joys of being women who love life and appreciate the value of friendships.

What is this sister/girlfriend thing really all about? Female bonding rituals have been around since before our grandmothers gathered to make quilts. Empty nesters take up hobbies easily shared in a group setting, and contemporary women get together to drink wine and invest money. No matter their lifestyles or ages, it's a thing only women get. Most men are clueless about our need to be together, but we were born with an innate understanding that our parents will die and our children will leave us, but our girlfriends will be around for the long haul. That is truly a thing worth celebrating!

I've been told that only those who have good relationships with their mothers are easily able to develop close and trusting relationships with other women. That isn't necessarily true—at least not in my case. I did not have a good relationship with my mother, but I do have great friendships—some going all the way back to my childhood. Just last week as I was leaving Lena's, my friend since I was nine and she was five years old, I told her that some of my other friends thought it was really neat that she and I had been friends since we were little girls. As I pulled away from her driveway, I heard her say, "We still are little girls." The sound of her laughter lingered, keeping me company on my drive home.

When I recently found myself at the airport with no ride home I called Lena. Without hesitation, she said, "I can do that," and in record time, she was there with a bottle of water and a snack to tide me over until we got out of the city and found our favorite restaurant. When I thanked her and told her I would make it up to her, she responded, "You already have, many times." I do hope that is true.

When I was younger and better looking, I might have (at least subconsciously) thought men were dispensable, but I have never had that attitude about my girlfriends. I knew if my child was sick, or a man had broken my heart, my friends would always be there with kind words, open arms, or a glass of wine, and sometimes all three. They would be ready to listen and help with whatever I needed.

One of my richest blessings is the diverse group of girlfriends I have. Some of them seem to have nothing in common but somehow we all get along. One friend in particular readily comes to mind— she hasn't been on time for anything since I've known her—but I love her. Her kind heart outweighs what is an annoying habit. (I'm sure some of my flaws would irritate a statue. How comforting it is to know that my friends will put up with me if I am a loyal friend who is accepting of them.)

A few years ago, my six-year-old twin grandchildren's dog had died, and it was quite traumatic because "ole Bob" had been around since before the kids were born. The whole family, but especially Chase and Chloe, were devastated.

I called the next day to see how they were doing. Chloe, in her sweet little quiet voice said, "Nana, did Mom tell you about Bob? Well, he died."

"Yes, I know, honey," I said, "and I'm so very sorry."

She answered, "That's okay, Nana, everybody has to do it and you'll probably be next."

I suppose that was a logical conclusion because I am the next oldest being in her world. I went to great lengths to explain that, in people years, Bob was about 95 years old and that, unlike Bob, my friend "Tweetie" was 95 and still healthy. I assured Chloe that I planned on being like Tweetie, which means I still had at least another 30 years. I belabored the subject further but my granddaughter remained clearly unconvinced.

Shortly thereafter, I showed Tweetie the article and photo about our "Ya Ya Sisters" Summer Solstice Celebration which was printed in the local mountain newspaper. She thought it looked like great fun and asked if she might join us the next year. Of course, I said yes, and before I knew it, she was shopping for a new hat to wear. She passed away three years later, still living alone in her own home.

My granddaughter was right. Everyone has to die. But I *do* hope she is wrong about my being the next in her world to go, and that I can continue, as they say in the Girl Scout song, to "Make new friends, but keep the old / One is silver, the other is gold."

The older I get, the more I value and appreciate these friendships; both new and old. When this life is all said and done, I'm convinced we will find that the sum total of all we are lies within whom we have helped and loved, and the people who loved us.

But I *still* plan on being like Tweetie.

RELIGION

Of all the mysteries in life, religion confuses me most. I get politics—don't *like* it, but I get it. Yet I fear I may never understand religion. People fight wars over it, argue about it over dinner tables, and in the name of love for the God in which they profess to believe, stir up more hatred because of it than just about anything else in existence.

If I had waited to join a church whose doctrines comprised all the things I believe I would never have joined any. The largest mystery is how anyone can be so arrogant as to imagine themselves the only person right about things that the most learned scholars are still pondering. How absolutely absurd!

I have never truly studied other religions with an open mind. From my observation, it appears that few other people have either. Most of us still believe–good or bad, right or wrong—the things we were taught as a child. My grandson pointed out to me that if we were born into a Muslim family we would be Muslims. If we had been born into a Jewish family we would be Jewish. Intelligent people know on a basic level that he is right but still we cling to the belief that it's our way and those who disagree will go to the hell we also believe in—whatever that means.

In all the years I've attended church and participated in Bible studies, I have become even more confused. The only thing I'm sure of is that I am in a place infinitely wonderful and that my role—at least the only effective one—is to be a fragment of the whole that, if I'm doing my best, may reflect some light into a dark place to help someone else on their journey. I believe that is the meaning of my life.

When I add up all my experiences with religion it spans more than sixty years, beginning with my first memory of my mother "getting saved" at a tent revival. It was the year after we moved out of the coal camp into and old abandoned farm house in the woods, miles up a dirt road "holler." I was bored and lonely, so when she suggested we all load up the car and go to the revival in a tent pitched in the ball field near our old school I was the first one in the car...

I don't remember what the preacher had to say but I thought the big white tent with light bulbs strung throughout was really neat. And it did have somewhat of a circus feel, punctuated by the screaming Baptist preacher.

About mid-way into the meeting, there was a fierce storm and the lights went out. From the pitch-blackness I heard a familiar voice.

"That's my mother!" I thought.

She was shouting things like, "Praise the Lord," over and over.

The next day she told us that she had been saved. (It looked to me like we had all been saved). She talked like a different person; she had completely stopped swearing. She even had a different look on her face—the anger, for the moment, was gone. The storm that moved through during the revival tent had moved out, taking with it the storm in our house.

But the storm that later came in a different form was far more devastating, at least to me. I was relieved to no longer be the victim of her screaming fits of rage but at some point I found being forgotten even more painful. I almost missed the beatings. She was so caught up in church and preachers that she forgot all of us. All of us, that is, except Shawn.

Mother must have taken him to every church meeting she could get to for miles—and by the time he was four years old, he would stand on a tree stump and preach a full sermon, complete with the sound effects common to Baptist preachers of the time.

It seemed that we lived in one church or another. She followed two or three of her favorite ministers to wherever they were preaching. During the services where she often sang solos, she kept up running cheer-like chants, calling out things like "Bless him, Lord" during the whole service.

I, on the other hand, barely understood a single word they said. The preacher paced back and forth behind the podium shouting out his message, and I think, quoting scripture, all the while taking out a damp handkerchief and wiping sweat away from his brow. The cadence would rise and fall according to the passion of the preacher with each sentence ending in a loud "hah" sound as he sucked in a large breath of air, enough to carry him through the next long sentence.

At the end of each sermon, on cue, the singing of "Just as I Am" would begin with the altar call. At this point, the fever pitch of the sermon had reached such a climax that someone, usually female and young (or female and sad and vulnerable) came forward and knelt at the altar where a few other parishioners were waiting and were joined by others who rushed forward praising the Lord. The praying would continue until the lost soul declared that he or she had been saved and the shouting would begin. A few weeks later a baptism would be scheduled. (Baptism was a vital event in the two-part "being saved" ritual necessary to ensure that you were indeed going to heaven.)

If the altar call didn't draw anyone down the aisle, the chorus would be repeated and, sometimes, the preacher would leave the pulpit and drape his arm around a certain sinner and plead with him or her to accept Jesus Christ right then! (I would have done most anything, and did, to escape the humiliation of being singled out in this way.)

The church Mother took us to also believed in what was called "backsliding." As I recall, when one returned to the Lord after backsliding it wasn't necessary to be baptized again. (Maybe I'm wrong, as each church seems to have a different policy on that.)

The older I became—with 12 being the magic number, the age of accountability—the harder the preachers begged me to come down to the altar, to stop resisting and answer the call of the Lord.

Eventually, in the middle of one summer night, as I tossed and turned in my misery, probably more from growing pains than religious conviction, I felt a sense of powerful relief from my emotional angst and declared that I had been saved. (More likely it was my way of escaping a public spectacle.)

The next morning after announcing to my family that I had accepted Jesus Christ as my savior I was sure that I would just float on air and even though I didn't need to break a cussing habit like my mother had, I surely would be transformed into a sweet girl filled with love and tolerance—things I definitely did not possess and was surely in need of. Like no longer being critical of my mother's table manners.

What an awful shock and disappointment when I sat down at lunch with mother and still found her to be rude! I couldn't stand to see people eat with their mouths open or hear them chew. I couldn't believe it still bothered me as much on that day as the day before! After all, I was supposed to be a changed person—filled with the Holy Spirit. I could not complain and give myself away as still being a sinner so I just sat very still, tears streaming down my face, pushing food around on my plate until I could escape unnoticed to my chores.

On the day of my baptism in the Big Jenny River, I remember my dad being somewhere watching. I looked up just before they dunked me under the water to see my best friend, Fern, standing on a bridge looking down at me. She was even more proud and stubborn than I was, and when I looked up at her I saw her hurry away—I think so that people wouldn't see her cry.

At that point, I did feel different and decided that maybe there was something to that religion thing after all. I studied the bible every day and must have read the first chapter of John a hundred times that year. I also enjoyed a sense of peace that had been missing all through my earlier teen-aged years.

I can't claim to understand God and religion anymore than I did back then, but somehow I've managed to build faith that there *is* a God and praying always affords me some measure of comfort.

But I cannot convince myself that what I believe is the only path to heaven. And I don't think I ever will.

FULL CIRCLE

$\mathcal{M}$y first husband George's last name was Hatfield—apropos because we lived in West Virginia. He always told me that his father was a direct descendant of Devil Anse Hatfield, leader of the famous Hatfields of the Hatfield-McCoy feud.

Though he was my brother Haford's best friend, I met George through my high school friend Fern, who was dating, and later married, his brother.

I didn't know it at the time but during high school, one of George's several part-time jobs was running gambling tables and selling moonshine in the basement of yet another brother's bar.

Because of the children, I kept George's last name after we divorced until I moved to Atlanta and remarried. I was often teased about the name—people nearly always asked if I was related to that infamous family. I usually answered no, but that my ex-husband was.

Fast forward and I'm living in Atlanta. I've just married my husband Gary, a retired federal agent who spent most of his career with ATF (Alcohol, Tobacco and Firearms).

My brother Haford decided to come for a visit and because he had once been close friends with George, I was a bit apprehensive about how well he would get along with my new husband.

So, I was nervous when after dinner one evening, conversation lagged. After an awkward pause, Haford finally spoke.

"Well, Sis," he said. "It looks like you've come full circle."

Confused, I looked at him. "What do you mean by that?"

"Well," he said, "You started out with a moonshiner and ended up with a damned ol' revenuer!"

A FEW MOMENTS OF FAME

*I*n my opinion, in every lifetime, there should be at least one moment of fame—large or small. Recognition is far more satisfying than monetary compensation could ever be. I have been fortunate enough to have had more than one of those moments. Most are attached to my career, and I have appreciated each as a measure of accomplishment.

When I was married to my first husband, George, it never occurred to me that I would ever need to earn a living. I wanted an education simply for self-satisfaction, and took classes at a local college for years. Some of those were night classes and several of my classmates were men taking advantage of the GI bill. I still loved my studies, even the classes that probably had no value in my future. But I loved learning new things.

When I realized that I had some natural talent for home decorating, I took a wonderful course offered by the New York School of Interior Design. I devoured each new subject and eagerly waited for the next assignment. I approached my studies as one might prepare for an exciting trip to some new and exotic place in a yet undiscovered part of the world.

Still the concept of using my education to earn money remained an unexplored possibility in my "safe" world. My *husband* was supposed to make the money. *My* job was to find ways to spend it.

(My creative talents were masterfully manifested in that category as well.)

I had fun helping friends with their decorating projects and even worked part time. I opened a small studio in partnership with another designer inside a local department store. Most of our business was window treatments—not a true test of our skills but great fun—and I took pride in having our small town newspaper print an advertisement and photo about our new business. But I never thought of it as a career—and my husband strongly objected to me working at all. (He later declared that was when all our marital problems began.)

So it was that a few years later, when I found myself facing life as a single parent, it didn't take long for me to realize that something had changed—work from that day forward would be a serious matter if we were to survive.

I sold our home and bought two older houses on a street across town. While still working in a department store, I remodeled those old houses and studied for my real estate license. My daughters and I lived on the premises of each while the work was being done. I would renovate and sell two more houses over the next seven years. As soon as one was completed and decorated, I had a huge party to show it off and, fortunately, every time, the party led to a sale.

I continued to try and sell real estate and decorate, but the economy was awful then, too—those were the days when mortgage interest rates rose to double digits and beyond. To make ends meet, I became a manufacturer's representative selling noise abatement and ventilation materials to West Virginia and Pennsylvania coal preparation plants.

There was a movement in the federal government to reduce the allowable noise level at the plants from 90 to 85 decibels. Anyone knowledgeable in the coal industry realized that the coal "barons" were too rich and powerful to lose that battle ultimately but they needed to make an attempt to appease the opposition. I knew most men who were already established as representatives would not be interested in learning a new trade and that the noise abatement business was only going to last a short time, so I would have little competition.

Before making the first sales call, and after I had thoroughly studied the nomenclature and my product, I dressed in my best suit and drove to Pittsburgh, Pennsylvania. Nervous, I went to the offices of Eastern Associated Coal, the largest company in Appalachia, and without an appointment, waited outside the senior buyer's office. At the end of the day, when he finally agreed to see me, I introduced myself, explained why I was there, and told him about my products. My purpose was to give him cause to remember me so that when orders showed up on his desk he might approve them. In retrospect, I realize how foolish I was. He would have remembered me for another reason. Just how many women would be doing that particular job? One—me!

Shortly after beginning that new career, I was interviewed by a reporter. A few weeks later, when I had almost forgotten about the interview, I opened the newspaper to find that I was the subject of a half page feature on the front page of the business section. The following week, I almost wrecked the car when, just as I touched my radio dial to change stations, I heard my own name on the news. The announcer was saying, "It seems that an attractive brunette has set out to silence the coal industry. Full story when we come back after a short commercial break."

Aluminized Polyester Panels Can Help

Woman Wants To Silence Coal

By Bob Stiegel
Staff Writer

Nadine Justice Hatfield would like to silence the coal industry once and for all.

Ms. Hatfield isn't a fanatical environmentalist. Neither is she an oil company stockholder or a nuclear power advocate. In fact, the attractive, 39-year-old Beckley woman is a coal miner's daughter, and proud of it.

"My dad (the late Curtis Justice) lost his arm in a mining accident when he was 24," says the Kopperston native. "But he loaded coal until he was in his 60s. I'd like to think I've got some of his traits in me."

Today, as president and sole employee of the fledgling Appalachian Kinetics Co., Ms. Hatfield believes she is "pioneering" noise and vibration control in West Virginia's coal industry.

The mother of two is a sales representative for Peabody Noise Control Co. (no relation to Peabody Coal Corp.), and is most usually seen on the state's highways, destined for coal mine sites where she'll expound on the virtues of baffles, curtains, enclosures, shock absorbers, and space age sounding materials like the neoprene-coated, fiberglass reinforced, aluminized polyester sound absorption panel.

"Coal companies have always tried ways to reduce noise and vibration," she says, "but before they've only had conventional methods to work with. The products I represent are the latest developments on products that used to be used only in other industries."

Ms. Hatfield, a former interior decorator who started her company six months ago, is targeting the state's scores of coal preparation plants for her products. With their clacketing conveyors, vibrating separation screens and deafening coal-car shakeouts, she says, prep plants are primed for a dose or two of modern noise deadeners.

"It's been kind of surprising, but I haven't had any trouble getting peo-

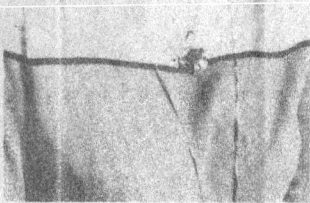

populated by males. "I guess it's because everyone knows noise is a problem."

Ms. Hatfield has sold to a trio of companies so far, she said, but one major coal company has been particularly enthusiastic, outfitting three of its prep plants with the Ki-

facilities in northern West Virginia, the entire room housing the coal shakeout is being paneled with the previously mentioned sound absorbing material. When completed, she said, the decibel level outside the shakeout will be reduced "from 100 to in the 70s, well below the 90

> 'Before I was an interior decorator. Can you believe that? I'm decorating the interiors of prep plants.'
>
> Nadine Hatfield

up and shake the coal out onto the conveyor," Ms. Hatfield, schooled by her father in mining techniques, said. "You can imagine how much noise that makes."

The same company is currently installing new shocks on vibrators at a southern West Virginia prep plant, she said. The shocks consists of heavy-duty airbags protected by steel sleeves, with the air pressure mechanically and constantly monitored, a vast improvement, Ms. Hatfield says, over the old, tire-like balloons.

"When they're installed you can note the effect immediately," she claims. "And the old shock absorbers are always blowing out and have to be changed. So this is something that adds to productivity."

Various other products are offered, ranging from barium-filled curtains to special foams, from damping compounds to a noise-swallowing material you can wrap around a particularly loud machine.

For the thoughtful employer who wants his control-monitoring employees to read their gauges in solitude, Ms. Hatfield has the solution: a completely enclosed double-wall steel structure that is perforated and filled with sound absorbing material.

"If we don't have a standard product for them," she notes, "I call in the engineers and we'll make it to their specifications."

Ms. Hatfield fully expects her business to blossom — "It has to, because noise control is something you have to deal with" — and said she's happy she changed vocations.

"I sold real estate for four years before I got into this," she says. "Before that I was an interior decorator. Can you believe that? I'm decorating the interiors of prep plants.

"There's a lot of pride in the coal industry, I saw that in my dad and I see it today. It's an interesting business, and it's filled with interesting people. I'm happy I'm involved in

---

In an effort to prove I had a real interest in learning exactly how my products were being used, I was obligated to accept an invitation to tour one of the deep mines. On the morning of the scheduled guided tour, I dressed in my standard work attire of yellow hard hat, blue jeans and western boots. I took a deep breath and headed for the coal mines to join my clients.

I felt guilty over my near panic attack due to claustrophobia—the prospect of going into the mines made me think of how my father might have suffered all the years he worked in them. When I arrived the men were waiting for me. They probably thought I would chicken out, but they didn't yet know me very well. I no longer cared if they were also whispering "nice ass" to each other behind my back—my only thought was in looking braver and more eager than I felt. Even so, I knew that I would not back out. I just hoped I wouldn't *pass* out at some point on the two-mile ride underground from the entrance to the seam of coal where the miners operated a continuous mining machine.

I was very pleasantly surprised. The large room was well lighted and had high ceilings. It was very noisy, but as the men pointed out the amazing operation, I was so enthralled I forgot to be afraid. They showed me how they hung the Brattice cloth to direct and redirect air flow from one area to another.

It was truly an incredible thing to witness and not at all like I had expected—I had been told stories about the early years, when my dad once had to work in mines so small the men had to crawl to the seam of coal. I must've proven myself tough enough for the guys. In retrospect, I'm sure that little tour won over my clients and resulted in future orders.

As soon as I was able to unload the last house I renovated, I moved away from West Virginia but have never forgotten that unique experience. However, to this day, I prefer dressing for work in lively colors, high heeled shoes and glitzy jewelry to wearing a hard hat, blue jeans and boots.

When I moved to Atlanta, I found that single parenting and making a living wasn't any easier there than they had been in West Virginia. I couldn't move the clients I had worked with and the only available design jobs I could find were in furniture sales for retail store owners. The jobs were no test of my design skills and they didn't pay as well, either.

A woman with whom I registered at an employment agency offered me a job in her company until I found a position with an

Atlanta design firm. I accepted but quickly learned that the promised sales position was not at all what she had presented.

After five grueling interviews with the executives of the largest temporary help agency in the world, I was hired as the branch manager. I had no clue what I was doing but was fearless in making some long overdue changes. I deleted 52 people from the work pool—some of which had been billing us and being paid weekly for months when they had never even shown up on the job site. Additionally, I dropped a few clients who were costing the temporary service more in worker's compensation than the profits made on their labor. At one time during the shake-up, a temporary worker's husband threatened my life and the security department posted a man outside my office door.

I missed decorating and didn't particularly like my strange new job, but the benefits were good and the pay was adequate—necessary evils for a single woman with a child to support. Even so, there were some memorable moments with that job as well.

An Atlanta-based national television network had a program on Saturday mornings called "Between the Lines," and they were doing a feature about local summer work for college students and anyone interested in temporary positions. My office was located in the heart of the city and because my boss was a man and the reporter preferred interviewing a woman, I was the logical choice. My part of the nationally televised show was seven minutes long and, much to my surprise, I found it a thoroughly enjoyable experience. I still have a video of the feature and occasionally show it to close friends, but only the ones who are sure to appreciate my interview and not comment on my 'big hair," which was common in the eighties.

Eventually I found a great job in my field at an upscale design firm located near my home. I was hired the same day of my very first interview which made me feel wanted and appreciated. As I was leaving that day, I overheard a future co-worker say, "I think you should hire the good looking one in the blue suit," and I knew I was going to be offered the job.

I was, and I loved getting dressed up every day to go to work in such a glamorous showroom. The art, furniture and accessories were of the finest quality and exquisitely displayed. There were individual mini-studios where each designer could set up presentation vignettes for our respective clients. It was wonderful to be able to work with other designers and bounce ideas off of them—a luxury I had never before experienced.

I went there expecting a competitive attitude but that was not at all what I found. I kept busy and somewhat to myself until one day when I was struggling to complete a presentation. When I realized I was running out of time, I approached a co-worker and asked for help. Immediately she called out to other available designers, "Nadine has a deadline for a client appointment and needs help."

Another person exclaimed, "Why didn't you tell us?" and in a few seconds three or four designers had gathered around me asking what I needed. All I said was, "I don't like this lamp with my scheme and can't seem to find the perfect fabric for accent pillows. Also, I could use another piece of art," and in a matter of minutes, my presentation was complete and I was calm and ready when my clients arrived.

We joked that we were like abused children who looked out for each other and banded together for protection—a reference to our very demanding boss. Sadly, I had never had to learn diplomacy or how to play politics, and did not do a good job of protecting myself.

In the first place, I had never had a boss in a creative position like this one. The owner of the company hired a flunky to drive her around and cater to providing whatever a diva like herself desired. In order to ensure the flunky's loyalty and attempt to compensate for the meager wages she paid, the owner gave her the title of "Design Coordinator," which she took very seriously and, unfortunately, abused.

I witnessed many occasions when young girls, hired straight out of design school, left in tears after only a few days. I had no respect for the woman and made the mistake of letting my feelings show. Usually, I ignored her and was successful enough that the owner allowed me to get away with it. But when the owner went out of town, I apparently said or did something that gave our "pseudo" manager the excuse she was waiting for. And she fired me.

At the time I didn't know I would probably be rehired the next day and was devastated over losing my beloved job. (I think I cried the entire night.) After that wake- up call, I was more careful but the damage was already done. Just when I became a bit too comfortable I was fired again. That time it stuck.

En route home, I remembered that I had never signed a "non-compete" contract, and started calling some of my favorite clients. I told them that I had had a parting of the ways with the design company and that I would love to continue working with each of them if they'd be comfortable with the arrangement.

One of my clients offered to cancel all orders they had already placed at that company and reorder from my new vendor. I knew I would never be paid the commissions I was due but, because there was always a risk that some of the carefully selected custom items would no longer be available, I advised them against it.

On the day all their furniture was scheduled for delivery, I had accumulated accessories and hired two men to assist me with the installation. The very heavy existing furniture on site had to be rearranged. I arrived early and waited for my helpers and the delivery truck. When my help didn't show up I had an awful creeping feeling of panic. When I called my guy, he reported that the other guy had the flu. "There is no point in my coming because I can't move all that stuff by myself," he said.

As I stood looking out the window thinking, "What am I going to do! This is my first project and I'm in real trouble here," the delivery truck from my old employer pulled into the driveway. The two young men I had met on many previous deliveries did not yet know I was no longer employed.

When I opened the front door, one of them said, "Miss Nadine, is there anything you want us to move before we bring in the new furniture?"

"As a matter of fact," I said, "There is an enormous bedroom ensemble that needs to be completely rearranged," which they cheerfully proceeded to do.

When everything new had been brought inside, I noticed that one of the new sofa cushions was missing. The lead delivery man called the showroom to inform them of the problem and asked that someone check the warehouse to see if they could locate the missing item. I heard him say, "No, June is not the designer for this job. Nadine is."

Again he argued, "No, I'm telling you Nadine is the designer, she's standing right here in front of me!" I so enjoyed the scenario that I could hardly wait for them to leave so I could laugh out loud.

I sprang into action placing accessories and hanging art. By the time the drapery people had arrived and installed the window and bed treatments, the delivery men had returned with the missing cushion. When my clients walked through the door of their newly decorated master suite, I greeted them with a glass of champagne and poured one for myself.

I kept all five of the clients I called that day, and my business grew rapidly. Each of those clients contributed greatly to the success I experienced—one offered money up front to purchase items I needed for their home and when the first project was complete paid me a handsome bonus to boot. Another client gave me referrals for what can only be called "dream" jobs. In every case we became good friends.

I needed and appreciated the income, but for me, the monetary compensation will never replace the accolades. I never get tired of replaying that scene at the end of a day of madly rushing around snapping directions (and often working harder than my younger assistants) when my client arrives and is thrilled with the results of my efforts. I'm so energized in those moments all of the earlier stress melts away.

In 1998 a client, whose home I had decorated six months earlier, called to inform me that the architect she used was being featured in *Better Homes and Gardens* magazine. She thought I would like to know that the photographer and journalists had been very complimentary of my work and asked permission to give them my name and contact information. Of course, I agreed.

A few days later, one of the editors called and did a lengthy telephone interview with me. As we were wrapping up the interview, she said "I think you'll be pleased—the photographs turned out great." I have always been skeptical regarding all areas of the media so I wasn't expecting anything worthwhile and was certain I would be misquoted.

The issue with this particular article was scheduled for release in about two months. A few days prior to the date it was due to hit the stands, I happened to be in a local pharmacy and checked in the magazine aisle on the chance that it had arrived early. There it was! I scarfed up several copies to share with family and friends.

I'm sure the other customers thought there was a crazy woman loose in the store. As I flipped through the pages and began reading the article, I kept exclaiming, "Oh, my gosh! Oh, my gosh!" I could hardly believe my eyes. They had quoted me verbatim and had included several photographs of my work—four pages in all. The article was supposed to have featured the architect. I had expected an honorable mention at best. Two years later a bathroom I designed featuring an elaborate stained glass window was included in a *Better Homes and Gardens* Special Interest publication.

Recently I was looking through a dated issue of *Atlanta Custom Home Builders* and thought it odd that I had kept it so long. As I always do

One of my room designs appearing as part of an
interior spread of *Better Homes & Gardens*, Fall 1998

before disposing of "shelter" magazines, I looked carefully through to see if there were any ideas I wanted to tear out and file before throwing it away. A picture of a basement and media room make-over caught my eye—it looked very familiar. It was a job I had done! No credits were noted and the homeowner's name wasn't revealed but there was no mistaking that it was one of my design jobs.

A famous man once said, "If you find a job you love, you will never work a day in your life." For me it was a long time coming, but I have had the good fortune to do just that. When friends ask when I plan to retire, I shake my head and smile.

"Never!" I exclaim. "Why would I do a thing like that?"

THE HOUSE AT DEBORDIEU COLONY

*I*n my opinion, it was the grandest house on the most exclusive stretch of private beach on the Atlantic coast. It wasn't my house but I had put my heart and soul into transforming it into a lovely and comfortable summer retreat for the owners.

In my work as an interior designer, I always put my entire being into every job and with each completed project I feel as if I have just given birth. The house at DeBordieu was no different—at least not in the beginning. But something changed along the way.

When people compliment my work, I just smile and tell them I pray a lot. They laugh and so do I, but I know it's true and I've never taken this God- given talent for granted. The accolades are usually followed by comments about how glamorous my work must be. Some of the stories I could tell would provide material for great entertainment but few of those behind-the-scenes episodes could be described as glamorous. The best example that comes to mind is the rental truck that backfired every five minutes en route home from a job.

When my husband of only a few years and I made a pit stop at the Social Circle exit, it was midnight. We were already exhausted and, needless to say, Gary was in an awful mood. For the entire six-hour trip he had constantly complained to me via cell phone about how miserable he was in that horrible truck. He cautioned me to stay close in my car because the truck was backfiring, "shaking him to pieces," and he was sure it was going to break down any minute. Before we pulled back onto the I-20 ramp, the alternator went out on my car. By the time AAA arrived, it was two o'clock in the morning. Now we were both in the infamous rental truck, which was still backfiring, following a wrecker through downtown Atlanta. This was one of the rare times my husband had not exaggerated. I kept thinking we would be mistaken for a drive-by shooter and were likely to encounter return fire before we got through town.

I laughed hysterically as I thought just how glamorous my clients would think my job was if only they could see me. I looked over at my tight-lipped new husband, who didn't seem to find our situation nearly as amusing as I did, and could see by the look on his face that the experience of this night had assaulted him with a clear and irrevocable refutation of any earlier ideas he might have had about life with a "sophisticated" decorator.

However, some parts of my work can be down right glitzy. For instance, a client whose home I had decorated in Atlanta called one day to say that they had just purchased property on the beach side of a development in South Carolina near their current, and more *casual*, summer house. As soon as I could get the new one ready, they said, they would move into it and use the old one as a rental and part-time guesthouse.

This was, unequivocally, the largest project I had been hired to do in years. They flew me over in a private jet to view the job site and to discuss my design vision and their needs for the new house. Upon arrival I found the exterior most impressive and tastefully landscaped. But that favorable first impression did a nose dive as soon as we stepped inside the front door. I cannot imagine what would possess anyone to paint all of the walls in the common areas of any house red, but especially in a beach house. To beach walkers at night, it must have looked like the place was on fire. Karen and I walked through every square inch of each level, talking non stop and making preliminary plans as we swept through the soon-to-be-empty rooms. On our return trip to Atlanta, I began making notes, asking questions like, "What is my deadline?" "When do you plan to arrive for the summer?"

She laughed at how big my eyes got when she said, "*Eight weeks.*"

"Surely you're joking," I said. "I don't know if I can do that but I'll try. You know I'll do my best."

The following Monday found me at the door of a wholesale furniture showroom at opening time. Fortunately, my usual salesperson was available and I immediately presented the dilemma, warning him that it might be a waste of his time pricing furniture unless we were able to find a manufacturer who could deliver before my deadline. (Otherwise, I would be forced to buy everything from local showrooms in South Carolina.) Amazingly, though, we found a high-end manufacturer offering exactly the style I was looking for that promised delivery in thirty business days. We spent most of the day together finalizing my selections.

The next day I took photographs, price quotes, and paint and fabric samples for my client's review and approval. She has always been able to make decisions quickly and, because I had worked with her before, I had learned her likes and dislikes—both critical factors to meeting the tight deadline. I then frantically set to work ordering furniture, accessories and fabrics.

In the meantime, my husband and I had already committed to a four-day Disney World trip with my sister and niece. I kept those plans in place, but explained to everyone that the only way I could go was with my cell phone attached to my ear. By the time we left for home again nearly all orders, which I knew from past experience needed a longer lead time, were placed and prepaid with specific instructions for delivery.

As soon as the previous owners had vacated the property, I arrived in South Carolina so I could begin hiring help and shopping for any items I needed to purchase locally. The minute I walked in the door on the main level of the house, I panicked. An enormous custom entertainment cabinet had been left in place because the movers couldn't get it out.

As I made my way upstairs I discovered another problem. The outdoor furniture for the two screened porches was gone. I had not ordered any because I had been told that these items were being negotiated into the sales contract.

I immediately called my client. "Oh my gosh," she said. "What are you going to do?"

After a long pause, I said "I don't know, but I'll figure it out." And I did.

I went to a store in Pawley's Island and selected furniture for the nanny's room and had it painted first so I would have a place to sleep. When the delivery truck arrived, I found they had sent four men. The first looked like a linebacker and must have weighed 300 pounds. Before he could ask where I wanted them to put the bedroom furniture, I said, "Do you know of anyone who might want these *beautiful* custom cabinets? I'm sure they cost a small fortune but my client doesn't want them, so I'm *giving* them away."

Just as he opened his mouth to answer, the other three men walked through the door. He turned to them instead, and said, "Look what she just gave me!"

After putting the new items in place, they spent the remainder of the afternoon disassembling the giant cabinet and hauled it away to the "linebacker's" house, where I'm sure it stands in a place of honor to this day.

Needless to say, as I continued in that fashion to dispose of other items from the soon-to-be rental house, I became very popular with the local delivery people. I never had to worry about the usual delays—my guys were always on time, and knew my name.

For the next five weeks, I worked from seven o'clock in the morning until midnight every day, not even taking time to walk on the beach. Still, it was too much work for me and my assistant, so I hired anyone available—even recruiting my husband, who made three trips from Atlanta bringing rental trucks filled with accessories. My best friend Lena took vacation time from her job at a bank to help me. (Not surprisingly, Lena was considerably more enthusiastic about her role than Gary was about his.)

When my client and her family arrived, the house was beautiful and complete to the last detail. I had even stocked the pantry and refrigerator with staple items and had music from *The Prince of Tides* playing in the background. They were so pleased with the results that I soon forgot my physical fatigue–it was quickly replaced with my own brand of excitement as I showed them around their newly decorated summer home.

Before leaving earlier that day, Lena had moved my personal belongings over to the old house, where I would spend one more night before going home to recharge and come back and prepare that house to be turned over to a rental agency.

Later that same summer I was invited to bring my family to the beach house when the owners planned to be away for a week. We had a great vacation together and it was fun for me to show some of my work to my children and grandchildren.

Three years later, my client decided to add two new towers to this already large house. Again I was flown down to check out the work in progress and to discuss a design plan for the addition. When the building project had progressed to a point where the general contractor was ready for me, I headed once again to South Carolina.

The deadline for this project was much longer. I could really enjoy the work and have time to appreciate my surroundings as well. On my long beach walks it gave me a start to look back at this grand house, which I used as a beacon. The exterior was dark tan stucco, not unlike the color of the sand. It appeared as if an elaborate sand castle had risen up as a monument to and continuation of the beach it sat upon.

In addition to attending to the design work for the new spaces, I also updated the décor in the original part of the house with new carpeting and replaced some items the contractors had ruined during the new construction. On some days I counted as many as 19 workers on site, which included the project manager, carpenters, helpers, and cleaning people. The young men began calling me "Miss Nadine." I couldn't finish a one-hour walk on the beach without being called with the crisis of the day, which sometimes was more unusual than one might think. I'll never forget one in particular. "Miss Nadine," said the voice on the end of the line, "call somebody quick, there's an alligator in the basement of the north tower."

I could hear the so-called grown men yelling like children. As soon as I was able to stop laughing I called the animal preservation people to come rescue the alligator and me. It was Memorial Day weekend so all the workers quit at noon and I was left to handle the situation alone.

I had never been in charge of anything like that and had no idea what to expect, but I hoped for something a little more official and scientific than what happened next. After waiting more than an hour I was surprised to see a red pick-up truck barrel up the driveway and come to a screeching halt inches from the garage door.

Out stepped a tall, middle aged man in boots, jeans and a ten gallon hat. This frustrated cowboy fished around in the back of his truck and pulled out a long stick with a loop of rope attached to the end. He then proceeded to lasso the alligator and after the reptile's jaws were secured, he slung it over his shoulder and into the back of his truck and then rode off into the sunset - I never saw him or the alligator again.

When work resumed the following Monday morning the "boys" had something new to talk about! In fact I'm betting it's still a topic of conversation for them.

Each day, I moved a Wave CD player to whatever area of the house I was working in so that I could listen to my favorite music. Among the workers there was one young man who stands out in my mind as a cut above the rest. Every morning he came in to say hello to me, but I remember one in particular.

"Miss Nadine," he said, "when we drove up today and I heard the music I knew you were here. I hope you don't mind but when you're gone I sometimes listen to your music and have come to like it. What do you call it?"

"It's classical, and a little light opera," I said. "A person can't live without Andrea Bocelli and Sarah Brightman, you know."

"Huh? Who?" he responded. "I don't think I've heard of them."

I don't know if my outward expression matched my broad inner smile but it pleased me greatly that I had influenced a trade-in of hard rock and country fare for classical music. Occasionally, I still think of that young man and wonder where he is now.

So many memories are attached to that design job, some frustrating, others amusing, but most are good memories. I came to love the DeBordieu house. I enjoyed the rare generosity extended to me by these very special clients who became my cherished friends. I didn't take it for granted but never imagined not being able to fall asleep again on the big bed-size porch swing, enveloped in a plethora of ocean sounds.

And then, one day, I received a call that the house had burned to the ground. Everything had been lost in the fire.

Karen was hurt and upset but thankful no one was injured. Though I did not offer protest when she said *it's just stuff, and things can be replaced* I knew that wasn't so. I thought about the one-of-a-kind furnishings, the rare art, the blown glass lamps I had ordered from Paris; the paintings I had commissioned, especially the 9' x 12' oil paintings that had graced the walls of the Casita bedrooms—one from a photograph I had taken at sunrise while the tracks of a Loggerhead turtle, who had just laid her eggs, were still fresh in the sand, the other from a photograph taken by the artist when he had flown down to the job site. It was a cloudy day and the white caps in the gray-green ocean blended perfectly into the colors on the horizon. The muted scene had created a serene and quiet repose for guests.

My husband cried when he heard the news. As usual, I did not. Instead, I simply set about helping my friends with the overwhelming process of creating an inventory list and replacement costs for their insurance claim, sometimes working until four o'clock in the morning.

When that daunting task was done, my client rented another house for a year and invited me to go and spend some time there. I thanked her profusely and began packing my bags. My husband and I took off for a week at the beach.

It was dark by the time we arrived and unloaded the car. Alone, I walked over to the beach with a flashlight and forced myself to look at the now empty lot. Still tears would not come. I stood on the small and blackened section of boardwalk that was still standing and, in a very utilitarian manner, thought, 'okay, that's *done*, now I can move on." Of course, I knew it wasn't, but other things needed my attention.

A few days later, in the daylight, I mustered up the courage to go back and walk over the charred pit where the house had once stood. I hoped I would find something tangible, an object I could hold in my hands, remnant of the time I had spent in this place I had loved.

I walked up the long and curvy still beautiful driveway and just as I neared the end, something caught my eye. Jutting up slightly out of the sand, shining in the sunlight, was the corner of a compact disc case. I kicked the sand from around it and first one and then another case was exposed. I picked them all up and was amazed to find that in one of the cases, the disc was unscratched. I remembered putting them in a drawer of the nightstand by the king size bed in the Casita. That room was located in the north tower to the far left of the driveway which was totally destroyed the night the house burned. I couldn't imagine how they somehow ended up buried in the sand on the opposite side. I was certain this was a gift left especially for me.

I raced back to the rental house, put the CD in the player, and began listening. It was the last of a three-album set—"Classical music for people who hate classical music," the very music the young man had come to appreciate. As I listened, I saw, in my mind's eye, the paintings—the purple and gold colors of the sunrise, the soft greens and gray hues of the beach on a cloudy day, the way sea shells float in shallow water as the tide moves in and ebbs out. The scenes in those paintings were etched in my mind. I had only hoped to find some small and tangible keepsake, but this was so much more.

Before the music stopped playing I realized there was another thing I had taken away from DeBordieu, something far more important and truly lasting—a thing that requires no maintenance, at least not the kind for which you need to hire a contractor. Instead, it is sustained by kindness, love, loyalty. It cannot be bought with money, is more beautiful than anything material, and nothing exceeds it in value, except family, perhaps.

I understood in that moment that beautiful objects were still objects, and therefore dead. Only people and the friendships between them matter...and friendship will never burn up in a fire!

SPRING DEER
Nadine Justice

Well, hello little deer.
Where have you been?
I've missed seeing you
pass by my house again.

Surely by now you see
we're closely related.
Your family, like me,
 could never be gated.

Like you, I'm scared too,
my deer little friend.
Not so sure about you
but know where I've been.

On your sad face
my own story I see.
So, I found this place
where we can all run free.

You knew it was this lady
who, on cold frosty morns,
left out for you and baby
those rare treats of corn.

Spring is in flurry
and food's aplenty.
No need to worry
'bout your wee family.

You all roam together;
 now you number five.
Have you ever seen another
 sitting here by my side?

No, it is only I
who waits all alone
unless you come by.
The lonely lady
in her house near the sky.

Visit me in spring this year
and when winter rolls around
I'll be waiting for you here;
a kindred spirit you have found.

BUILDING THE MOUNTAIN HOUSE

"**W**alter," I said, "I think it's great that you're enjoying your new mountain retreat, but could we please get back to writing up my order. I have another appointment in Buckhead in an hour." Walter was my sales representative at Mayo Wholesale Furniture. During the many years we had done business together, we had become close friends.

He was eager to share his good news with me, but except for being happy for him, I had no interest in property in the north Georgia mountains. However, as he expounded on the great buy he had found and how there was another building lot across the road from his place, my interest was piqued—so much that my husband and I found ourselves standing on that mountain lot the following Sunday afternoon.

The one across the street from Walter's had sold the day before we arrived, but "Mountain Man Dan," the real estate agent, pointed out the adjoining lot, which was offered at an even better price. Gary and I walked around checking out its amazing view, and finally, I asked him, "Do you like it?"

Needless to say, he answered affirmatively, and I turned to Dan and said, "We'll take it." I heard a gasp from my husband, who wasn't accustomed to making on-the-spot decisions. We proceeded to follow Dan to his 180-year-old log cabin to write up the contract. During the process, he and I exchanged information about our Kentucky heritages and discovered we were distant cousins.

The purchase of that mountain lot was intended to be strictly an investment and nothing more. A year or so later I began designing a little cottage I visualized as perfect for the setting. The idea took hold of me like a disease, and before I knew it, I found myself spending every spare moment studying all the textbooks on building I could get my hands on. I showed my drawings and sketches to Gary and he kept telling me that since I had to oversee building and remodeling jobs for my clients all the time, I should do it for myself. When I was finally sure that I could make it happen, I began searching for the best local subcontractors and threw myself into the most difficult and ultimately most rewarding project of my life.

We learned about another house in the same development that had been on the market for several months. The owner was eager to rent it because there had been little interest from potential buyers and I needed a place to stay one or two nights per week. Located in a ravine where it was not visible from most other houses, the house was painted a distinct blue color, including porches and trim. The neighbors had already nicknamed it "The Smurf House." The most difficult part of the entire building project for me were the nights I spent there—I was too scared to relax enough to fall asleep and too embarrassed to admit it and ask for help or company.

A man named Buddy had worked for me for several years, assisting with installations in my design business. He had far more experience than I did with projects of this size so I decided that as long as he was available to pitch in or offer advice, I was safe to undertake such an overwhelming task. But as fate would have it, shortly after the site work was completed and the foundation had been laid, Buddy's wife called to tell me that he'd injured his eye on another job and was going to need a cornea transplant. Though

I was concerned about him and his family, I must admit that I was also stressing about how I could manage the house without his help.

I had hired a good framer, a great plumber, the best electrician around and a skilled carpenter, but finding general laborers was a real challenge. Every time I found a good old mountain boy and things were clipping along, hunting season would roll around and progress on the house would come to a screeching halt. One young man I interviewed said "Well, ma'am, I hate to turn down work, but it's huntin' season."

On one disappointing trip, my husband came along for a rare visit. That particular week, it was difficult to tell if anything had happened at all and some of the work had not been done according to my instructions. I was so discouraged that I called Buddy, because his mother had at one time expressed an interest in buying the place. I told him to let her know I was ready to sell. "Nadine," he said, "if you give up now you'll hate yourself later."

I then turned to my husband who had remained uninvolved to this point, and said, "I need your help. I can't do this by myself." He responded by reminding me that it was *my* project and that I was the general contractor and *he* knew nothing about building a house. He told me that I shouldn't have started the project with the expectation of getting him involved when it became too much to handle. I retorted, "Okay, fine! When it's finished I don't want to see you park yourself on *my* back porch."

We now laugh about that Sunday afternoon meltdown because we both love the house, which turned out even better than my expectations. On summer nights, we argue over who gets to sleep on the screened porch sofa.

The mountain house is where I go now to recharge when work has worn me down. It's the sanctuary I've used to write these memoirs, the place I escape to be alone when I'm sad or worried about a friend or family member, the retreat I use for praying when I'm scared.

Only a 90-minute drive from our "city house," it might as well be a world away. The local culture is slow-paced and casual, offering free concerts at the historic downtown courthouse on Friday nights, festivals in the city park, and a slew of antique shops and blue grass music. A large number of people have moved after retirement to these mountains to write or paint — things they wanted to do but put on the back burner until their "careers" were over.

The mountain house came with a few other unexpected benefits. When I'm at a bluegrass concert in the area, and the banjo picker is good enough, I can close my eyes and imagine he is Poppy George and I'm a child again sitting on my grandparent's front porch in Kentucky.

Even the drive offers a chance for me to vicariously make up for a few regrets about things I wish I had done when I was a young woman. It doesn't bother me so much that I can't ride a bicycle, but how I wish I had learned to ride a motorcycle! As the riders whip past me on Blood Mountain, I picture myself as a young woman again, with my black hair flying free, riding on my own blue Harley and leaning into each of the 320 curves. When I still lived in the West Virginia mountains, I found that a long drive on one of the big mountains could clear my head and calm my nerves. Now, I drive like a race car driver on the curvy mountain roads that carry me to this special place I have come to love and appreciate.

For when I arrive, I am instantly transformed. Every time I look through the windows of the A-frame wall, I lose myself in the midst of the mountains that enclose me in their arms and protect me. And the breathtaking view of the distant mountains from the back porch melts the burdens of my everyday life away.

It has been seven years now since we moved into this "weekend retreat," and though I know there will come a time when Gary and I will be too old to maintain two houses, I thank God for it now — and for Buddy, for encouraging me to not give up on it.

THEN AND NOW

I went to a formal dinner party several years ago hosted by a lovely lady who had told me privately that her father, like mine, was a coal miner from West Virginia. During dinner conversation regarding the respective guests' backgrounds, she curiously left out that particular detail. It appeared as if she was embarrassed about her father.

I have never been ashamed of my father's career as a coal miner. In fact, my admiration of his character and courage has instilled in me a deep feeling of pride and a fierce sense of loyalty to the hard-working coal mining families in Appalachia.

When I decided on the title for this book, I thought *I'm A Coal Miner's Daughter But I Cain't Sang* was catchy and funny, but it was also apropos. Despite the sudden and short-lived harmony that came forth from my throat in my mother's hospital room, I can't carry a tune well enough to muddle through hymns in church. My mother sang solos, my sister has a very nice singing voice, and my younger brother's a capella rendition of "Wayfaring Stranger" at Mother's funeral was the most beautiful thing I have ever heard. I never once heard my father sing but he whistled as he worked. I can't even whistle a recognizable tune!

I've heard the rumors and jokes about people from Appalachia, but the members of my family, in my opinion, were some of the most intelligent and resourceful people I have ever met. I am forever indebted to them all, especially my mother and father, for any successes I am able to claim. It was therefore not my intention to ridicule the colloquial language of another coal miner's daughter. Instead, I chose the title mostly out of respect for the language I grew up with. Those are my people—I understand them.

My life in Atlanta can, at times, feel a lifetime removed from my roots. However, I never forget where I came from and I never forget to be grateful that, because of the sacrifices they made for their children, our lives will never be as difficult. All four of Curtis' and Nell Ruth's children have done well in life and all of our children are doing even better.

I know where that began.

Who Am I?

By Nadine Justice

I glance in the dimly lit mirror;
dim is exactly the way I like mirrors now.
Turning my head from side to side,
I try hard to glean some evidence of the young girl
I once was.
"There," I say, "She's still in there," only
faintly peaking through the clear and strong version
of the woman I have become.
"Good riddance" I say. "I never liked her anyway,
I'll gladly leave her behind." …
Until
I move closer and remember that wounded little girl
and how she got to be someone
I didn't want tagging along on this journey.
Closer yet and I catch a few slim glimmers of her,
lost and searching for a home. I move my face into
the reflection and decide I do like that girl.
With compassion and love she never had, I take her
trembling hand and bring her along,
wounded soul, scars and all.
I embrace and mesh the girl into the me I have become,
and know that I cannot be one without the other.
Finally, who I was and who I am are one,
almost whole, person.
I will never abandon her again.

The Appalachian VOICE

15 years in print and still **FREE**

February / March 2012

Then & Now

Forty years ago, a wave of coal slurry swept away communities along Buffalo Creek, killing 125. Some problems from our past have improved — others seem stuck in time. Have we learned our lesson?

ALSO INSIDE: The Habits of Hibernating Bears • Georgia's Historic Blood Mountain • Standing Up for Clean Water

AFTERWORD

As I said in the beginning, the memories of the awful hardships suffered by those coal-mining families still haunt me. I was living in Turkey in 1972 when the Buffalo Creek flood happened. The news reached us by way of week-old *Time* and *Newsweek* magazines, followed by long letters from my family. One told a story of a distant cousin who walked, half-crazed, through the mountains for nearly forty miles to reach the safety of a relative's home after watching his wife and their home swept away by the black water.

In early 2012, an article about the flood and the Buffalo Creek area 40 years later appeared in *The Appalachian VOICE*. Following are excerpts from that article by staff writer Brian Sewell:

"Those who cannot learn from history are doomed to repeat it."
– George Santayana

"In the morning of Feb, 26, 1972, nearly 132 million gallons of water and coal waste rushed from Buffalo Mining Company's slurry impoundments through Buffalo Creek Hollow, Logan County, W.Va. The flood coursed through 16 coal mining settlements along the creek where hundreds of families lived, while children slept or watched cartoons as their mothers cooked breakfast. In an instant their lives were washed away … The company men of Pittston Coal called it an "act of God." …

A series of three dams were built on the Middle Fork upstream from the Buffalo Mining Co. tipple in the 1950s and 60s as Logan County continued to grow as one of southern West Virginia's prolific coal-producing counties. Dam No. 3, the largest, stood 60 feet above the pond and downstream dams below. When it gave way, the others collapsed instantly.

Rushing through Buffalo Creek hollow, the slurry carried with it semi-rotten trees, rocks and sediment. It ripped homes from their foundations and swept up cars and bridges until it finished three hours and 15 miles later at Guyandotte River, destroying nearly everything in its path. When the physical chaos settled, out of a population of 5,000 people, 125 were killed, 1,121 injured, and more than 4,000 were left homeless. ...

... The state's Public Services Commission, responsible for dams blocking streams, required detailed plans for any structure over 15 feet high that obstructed a waterway. In the case of dams above Buffalo Creek, no plans were submitted. "They just ignored the law," says [Jack] Spadaro [engineer hired to investigate the disaster]. "But the Public Service Commission and the prosecutor in Logan County decided that since the dam was already built, they couldn't do anything about it." ...

... On Oct. 11, 2000, it happened again. Around midnight, a portion of the Martin County Coal Corporation's Big Branch impoundment near Inez, Ky. collapsed, inundating two tributaries of the Tug Fork with 306 million gallons of sludge. The EPA called it the worst [environmental] disaster in the southeastern United States, but luckily this time, no one was killed ..."

After my mother died, I found a 1985 article, in one of her old hat boxes, about the long history of labor/management clashes affecting the lives of miners and their families.

'It's The Same Fight Today.'

UMWA HISTORY

This year is not the first time that coal miners have had to fight for their union in the Tug River Valley, on the West Virginia-Kentucky line.

Over 60 years ago, one of the biggest battles in UMWA history occurred in the same area where union members are now fighting A. T. Massey Coal Co. for a new contract.

Then, as now, the area was under seige by armed thugs hired by coal operators to break the UMWA.

Then, as now, miners' children lived in fear.

"How can you forget?" says Bertha Collins Damron, now 66, of North Matewan, W. Va.

At three years old, she clung to her mother's skirts as state militia stormed their home and ransacked their belongings.

They were looking for her father, union leader John Collins, who "laid up in the mountains night and day fighting for the union.

"We never saw him, but we knew he was fighting for us, so we could have a better life," she said.

"And it breaks my heart to see these boys having to go through that hardship all over again. I tell my children, 'History is repeating itself, but we have to fight for our freedom.' "

Fighting Company Violence
The battle for union recognition in southern West Virginia heated up after World War I, when the UMWA targeted non-union Mingo County and the coal operators vowed to break the union movement.

Guards from the notorious Baldwin-Felts agency evicted union families at gunpoint from their company-owned houses, and roamed the mountains hunting down UMWA organizers.

For survival, union families set up large "tent colonies."

But an anti-union governor declared martial law to "preserve the peace" and sent in state militia, who ripped through miners' tents, smashed furniture, and in one case shot a UMWA member at point-blank range.

Company terrorism increased and, on May 19, 1920, a gunfight broke out in Matewan, W. Va., that left seven Baldwin-Felts thugs, and the town's mayor and two other union men, dead.

Union leader Sid Hatfield, Matewan chief of police, was one of 16 UMWA members charged with murder in the "Matewan Massacre."

Hatfield and the others were acquitted by a Mingo County jury, but later framed and charged in neighboring McDowell County.

On Aug. 1, 1921, as they were climbing the steps of the county courthouse in Welch with their wives, Hatfield and Ed Chambers, another union leader, were shot and killed by Baldwin-Felts agents.

The murders of Hatfield and Chambers by company guards caused a public outcry and brought an outpouring of support for the miners both from the Tug Valley communities and other local unions.

Building Support
Under seige by the thugs and the state militia, miners and their families banded together for survival.

"It's like what's happening now," said Mrs. Damron. "The whole community stood up strong for the union, even the most prominent business people. If they hadn't, we would never have made it.

"But back then, after the governor put in martial law, people had to help out undercover. They'd arrest two people for just standing and talking out in public."

But that didn't stop the miners' families and friends.

"There was always a way," she said. "We'd always get help to the people who needed it."

Showing Solidarity
As reports of company violence spread to surrounding UMWA districts, local unions organized immediate support for their brothers in Mingo County.

Delegates to a District 17 convention voted to send 50 organizers into the area.

Local unions collected badly needed supplies to send to striking families.

Miners from other areas travelled to Mingo County to lend their support, and those who couldn't travel mounted a campaign to bring the strike to public attention.

Union leader Sid Hatfield, 1894-1921

April-May 1985   United Mine Workers Journal

To this day, there is a feeling among coal mining families that nothing much has changed by any account. The following article from Open Salon* in 2010 is yet another example of "then and now."

It's Happening Now:
The 2nd Battle of Blair Mountain

JANUARY 31, 2010 12:46PM — West Virginia Mountains. It is a battle whose ugly scars may be permanent. It is a battle being fought on hallowed ground, where 88 years ago more than a hundred desperate and angry men gave their lives for the chance to live with dignity. Raging now in southwestern West Virginia is the second Battle of Blair Mountain.

First some background. If you've read my blog before, some of this may be familiar. In the immediate years following World War I, miners in West Virginia began organizing for better wages and living conditions under the auspices of the United Mine Workers Union. For years, much of the state had been mired in a seemingly endless cycle of poverty, where men – and boys – worked in incredibly dangerous conditions not for dollars, but for script, faux money that could only be used in stores owned and operated by the coal companies for which they worked. Making matters worse, the companies owned the land and forced workers to rent ramshackle houses from their employers. The companies were the only landowners and landlords around ...

*http://open.salon.com/blog/procopius/2010/01/30/its_happening_now_the_2nd_ battle_of_blair_mountain

Coal mining town of Blair Mountain in the 1920's

On August 1, 1921, Sid Hatfield, the police chief of Matewan, West Virginia, was gunned down in front of the courthouse in the town of Welch, West Virginia, by gunmen believed to have been hired by the Baldwin-Phelps Detective Agency. It was a revenge killing, since Hatfield had supported the strikers during the early skirmishes with the Baldwin-Phelps agents. Enraged at Hatfield's murder, between 10,000 and 15,000 angry miners began marching toward Logan and Mingo Counties to organize a union by force. In their eagerness to avenge Hatfield's murder, some of the marching miners even hijacked a freight train, which alarmed authorities as far away as Washington, DC.

As news of the approaching mob of miners reached officials in Logan County, the county sheriff, with the support of the Logan County Coal Operators Association, set up 10 miles of defensive positions around Blair Mountain. As the miners grew near, some 2,000 heavily armed private security forces, including many with machine guns, prepared for battle. Fearing a bloodbath, many of the miners decided to halt the march and negotiate with authorities in neighboring Boone County. On August 26, most of the miners started to return home. The sheriff of Logan County, however, would not be denied his battle. Sharpshooters began firing on many of the miners even though they had discontinued their march and were heading home. Several innocent bystanders, including women and children, were caught in the crossfire.

Now enraged, the miners turned around and resumed their march on Logan County. More trains were hijacked. On August 29, a full scale battle commenced. It was not only the private security forces facing the miners. President Warren G. Harding authorized World War I hero Gen. Billy Mitchell to use surplus airplanes and munitions from the war to make air strikes against the miners, dropping bombs as well as gas on several locations near the town of Jeffrey, West Virginia. This marked the only time in American history that air power was used on American soil against American citizens.

The battle lasted close to a week. On Sept. 2, Federal ground troops arrived in Logan County. With that, the miners called off their efforts and began to return home. The Battle of Blair Mountain was over. With more than 100 killed, and nearly 1,000 injured, it was the bloodiest insurrection to take place in the United States since the Civil War. For the miners, this attempt to unionize ended in failure.

Move the clock forward 88 years. On March 30, 2009, after years of efforts by various interest groups and preservationists, Blair Mountain was added to the National Register of Historic Places, to be managed by the National Park Service. This was good news for a variety of reasons. First, as a significant historical site, inclusion in the Registry gives the nearly forgotten events of 1921 much deserved recognition. Perhaps more important than that, however, is the fact that its status as a national historical site will protect Blair Mountain from the potential ravages of mountaintop removal coal mining. Already, the tops of several neighboring mountains have been blasted away, leaving a permanent scar on what was once an undeniably beautiful landscape.

With its listing on the National Historical Register, Blair Mountain will be spared that fate.

Wrong!

Inexplicably, on December 9, 2009, Blair Mountain was delisted from the National Historical Registry. According to a spokesperson for the West Virginia State Historical Preservation Office (SHPO), the delisting resulted from concerns expressed by a majority of property owners on the site, as well as objections from three coal companies headquartered out of state that covet the mountain's underground riches.

In advocating Blair Mountain's delisting, the SHPO claimed there were 57 landowners on the site, of whom 30 voiced objections to its inclusion on the Historical Registry. However, supporters of the historical designation have identified 61 landowners, and only 25 legitimate objectors, a far cry from the majority that the SHPO claims objects to the historical designation. In addition, two of the so-called objectors have been deceased for several years. When asked about that, the State Historical Preservation Officer (SHPO) replied, "We cannot confirm or deny that there are no deceased on the SHPO list dated May 21, 2009."

For a place with as much historical significance as Blair Mountain, there has been very little in the way of archeological exploration of the site. In 2006, the first methodical archeological field survey took place under the auspices of Appalachian State University. After three weeks in the field, hundreds of artifacts were found, including a large number of shell casings and rifle bullets. A few guns were found, as well. Some of the discoveries suggest that the miners came much closer to realizing their goal of reaching the town of Logan than had been previously assumed. More in depth analysis of the site could almost certainly help historians piece together the events of that bloody week to reach a better understanding of what actually transpired.

The removal of Blair Mountain from the National Register of Historic Places makes that possibility much more difficult, if not impossible. In 2006, before Blair Mountain was included on the Registry, The National Trust for Historical Preservation listed the battle site as one of the 11 most endangered historical sites in the nation. If the coal companies succeed in keeping Blair Mountain off of the Registry, this will be the mountain's likely fate:

Those who refuse to sit quietly while powerful political and economic forces seek to reap short-term profits at the expense of historical and scenic preservation are fighting back. They have formed a non-profit advocacy group called The Friends of Blair Mountain (www.FriendsOfBlairMountain.org). Their struggle to save this important site is a battle every bit as consequential as that which was waged in August, 1921. The 2nd Battle of Blair Mountain has commenced. Its outcome is uncertain.

Maybe those reporters were right, and nothing *has* changed. And nothing will, if the people who love that beautiful land give up on it. Now when I go back to West Virginia, I either stay with my friend Jessica near Lewisburg or with my cousin Georgia Marie in Beckley. On my way home there is a place the locals call "the split" where I-64 and I-77 separate. No matter how many times I drive that route it takes my breath away. I've seen a lot of mountains in my lifetime, including the Colorado and Canadian Rockies, and I've flown over Mont Blanc, but if there's a prettier place on this earth, I've yet to see it. I would like to believe that when I'm long gone, Sarah, Marshall, Zachary, Chase and Chloe, and *their* grandchildren will be able to see those wild and wonderful West Virginia mountains exactly the way I do now—that it will never change.

Outside of my work, I focus on spending time with my grandchildren, and have started a second book. But I will make time to stand up in an effort to save Blair Mountain. I don't have an ounce of the musical talent of Kathy Mattea or the late Hazel Dickens, but that won't stop me.

I "cain't sang," but that doesn't matter. My voice *will* be heard.

ABOUT THE AUTHOR

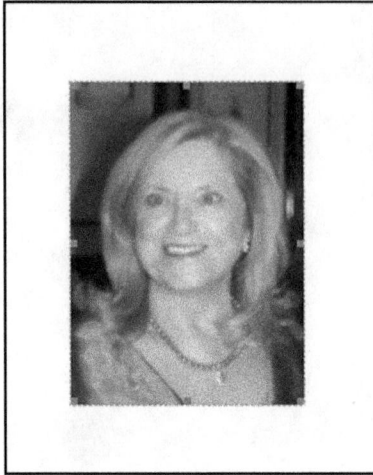

Nadine Justice divides her time between a mountain-top cottage in Blairsville and her home in Atlanta. An interior designer by training, her work has been published twice in *Better Homes and Gardens* and in *Atlanta Custom Home* magazines. Though *I'm a Coal Miner's Daughter... But I Cain't Sang* is her first book, two of the stories told within have been published in an anthology by the Georgia Mountain Writers Club. Married for the past 15 years to a retired federal agent, Nadine enjoys spending time with her four "perfect" grandchildren.

To order additional copies of

I'm a Coal Miner's Daughter...But I Cain't Sang

email the author at
nadine@unitedwriterspress.com

www.ingramcontent.com/pod-product-compliance
Lightning Source LLC
Chambersburg PA
CBHW051957090426
42741CB00008B/1430